Urban Marginalisation in South Asia

The community of waste pickers in Calcutta stands on its own against the hostile outside which comprises the state, elites and mainstream society. The residents of this unique world continuously try to escape the 'ideal' world of uniform homogeneity of legally legitimate profession, shelter, sanitation, education, healthcare, savings, credit and cultural activities of the mainstream.

This book examines the lives and society of a marginalised urban community of waste pickers living within the city of Calcutta, and yet on the periphery of mainstream society. Through interpretive ethnography of the studied community focusing on ideological marginalisation, as distinct from economic marginalisation, the book studies the community and their world. It uniquely presents a volume of work in the field of ideological or socio-cultural marginalisation: showing how and why socio-cultural marginalisation is expressed through the daily experiences of material and emotional dilapidation, and physical and socio-cultural seclusion as experienced by the waste picking community in Calcutta. It provides an extensive and intimate discourse on the decay of the soul and mind, breakdown of the interpersonal and neighbourhood ties through the mediation of the biased state, mainstream and elite policies attached with the defamed peripheral regions of the city. It argues that ideological marginalisation represents alternative resistance to exploitation through silent defiance, non-participation and non-cooperation by the marginalised people with mainstream society, state and non-governmental organisations (NGOs). It concludes that there is a large scope for studying the negotiation skills of waste pickers/marginalised people in terms of their business with their retailers which help them attain some economic returns, although they still lack social capital, networking skills and human capital.

Presenting exciting new ethnography against the background of important theoretical concepts, the book initiates a dialogue about options for a change in the situation of these marginalised people vis-à-vis the state, elites and mainstream society. It will be of interest to an interdisciplinary audience in the fields of Social and Cultural Anthropology, Urban Studies, Development Studies, Urban Sociology and South Asian Studies.

Nandini Sen received her PhD from Goethe University, Frankfurt/Main, Germany.

Routledge/Edinburgh South Asian Studies Series

Series Editor:
Crispin Bates and the Editorial Committee of the Centre for South Asian Studies, Edinburgh University, UK.

The Routledge/Edinburgh South Asian Studies Series is published in association with the Centre for South Asian Studies, Edinburgh University – one of the leading centres for South Asian Studies in the UK with a strong interdisciplinary focus. This series presents research monographs and high-quality edited volumes as well as textbooks on topics concerning the Indian subcontinent from the modern period to contemporary times. It aims to advance understanding of the key issues in the study of South Asia, and contributions include works by experts in the social sciences and the humanities. In accordance with the academic traditions of Edinburgh, we particularly welcome submissions which emphasise the social in South Asian history, politics, sociology and anthropology, based upon thick description of empirical reality, generalised to provide original and broadly applicable conclusions.

The series welcomes new submissions from young researchers as well as established scholars working on South Asia, from any disciplinary perspective.

Activism and Agency in India
Nurturing resistance in the tea plantations
Supurna Banerjee

Everyday State and Politics in India
Government in the Backyard in Kalahandi
Sailen Routray

Neoliberalism and the Transforming Left in India
A contradictory manifesto
Ritanjan Das

Urban Marginalisation in South Asia
Waste Pickers in Calcutta
Nandini Sen

www.routledge.com/asianstudies/series/RESAS

Urban Marginalisation in South Asia

Waste Pickers in Calcutta

Nandini Sen

Routledge
Taylor & Francis Group
LONDON AND NEW YORK

First published 2018 by Routledge

2 Park Square, Milton Park, Abingdon, Oxfordshire OX14 4RN
52 Vanderbilt Avenue, New York, NY 10017

Routledge is an imprint of the Taylor & Francis Group, an informa business

First issued in paperback 2020

British Library Cataloguing-in-Publication Data
A catalogue record for this book is available from the British Library

Library of Congress Cataloging-in-Publication Data
A catalog record has been requested for this book

ISBN: 978-0-8153-5766-7 (hbk)
ISBN: 978-0-367-58973-8 (pbk)

Typeset in Times New Roman
by Wearset Ltd, Boldon, Tyne and Wear

Contents

Acknowledgements

This book is dedicated to the waste picker community in Calcutta. They helped, shaped and supported the ethnography and the whole research concept behind it. This book would not have been possible without them.

I am sincerely grateful to my academic supervisor Professor Dr Susanne Schroeter (Institute of Ethnologie, Goethe University, Frankfurt Am Main) for providing me the precious opportunity to work towards a Ph.D., her knowledgeable and thought-provoking advice, comments and criticism. Throughout the past few years she has guided me in repeatedly revising my research ideas and writing towards continuous betterment. Her visits and lectures, both in different universities in Calcutta, India and in my field areas, were important for this book.

I remain indebted to Goethe University of Frankfurt for giving me the chance to complete my thesis. I do not know how to thank Mr Oliver Bertrand enough for his kind and generous support with all official and technical sustenance; starting from university admission to fieldwork and official networking. I am immensely grateful to Mr Gunnar Stange for his affectionate understanding and providing me with his thoughtful friendship and shelter. I must mention Roman in this regard as well. He still remembers and preserves his underpants which I burned to cover the strong light in the room. I experienced a friendly and loving atmosphere in the Department of Anthropology, and I sincerely thank all my research colleagues for this.

I owe very much to Professor Dr Alexander Law, Sociology Department, School of Social and Health Sciences, University of Abertay, Dundee. Professor Law has always extended his time and willingness to discuss academic problems concerning this book and in due course became my second academic supervisor. His insightful advice profoundly enriched my thought process.

I wish to acknowledge my obligation to Professor Crispin Bates (Professor of Modern and Contemporary South Asian History, Department of History, School of Social and Political Science, University of Edinburgh) for his criticism, and particularly for improvements of phrases and grammatical constructions. He also deserves my appreciation for his kind inclusion of me within the network of the Centre for South Asian Studies and for providing me with the opportunity to publish the book as part of the Routledge series.

My late parents, Ms Gopa Sen and Dr Kalyanmay Sen, who always encouraged me towards academic research deserve a special mention. It is a great pity that when I have finally found an interest in research, they are not alive to share my joy. However, my partner Professor Dr Arnab Bhattacharjee (Department of Economics, Heriot-Watt University) took up the task of driving me to complete my thesis. Hence, I dedicate this book to him too, who all along invested his trust, his knowledge, anger and many other strong emotions in me.

My deep gratitude is extended to my warm comrade and friend Dr Carlo Morelli (Economics Department, University of Dundee) for handling my nervousness sensibly and lending his attention and time to argue with me. His patience and criticisms helped to shape my thesis. Carlo made me think about the real harsh and indelicate aspects of marginalisation through different discussions and readings.

I am gravely saddened that my main field logistics provider during both field works (2011–13) and long-time friend, the late Mr Haider Ali (the Chief Functionary of Tiljala Society for Human and Educational Development), is no longer among us. I pay my tribute and homage to him by completing this book. He was like my father figure. I am sincerely obliged to all my Tiljala Society for Human and Educational Development (T-SHED) friends and informants. Especially Mr Alamgir, Ms Krishna Chowdhury, Ms Mita Nath, Ms Rubina Hussain, Ms Kashmira Khatoon, Ms Ujjala, Ms Heera Ghosh, Mr Jasim, Mr Debasish Panda and Ms Karabi Roy Chowdhury (for being my hostess during my field work) for their kind cooperation and continuous assistance in building up a network with the waste picking community, State Conservancy Section and corporate sector.

My thanks to Dr Subrata Bagchi for his kind assistance during fieldwork and for taking photographs and conducting interviews during a massive fire which destroyed a huge number of the shelters of the waste picking community (as I could not attend this tragic crisis). He supported and helped me to organise seminars for my supervisor, Professor Susanne Schroeter.

Thanks are due also to Mr Partha Dey (India) and Dr Alexis Wearmouth (UK) for capturing some of the brilliant photos of the daily life of the community during my fieldwork.

I acknowledge all my well-wishers, especially Dr Bishakha Roy (for being a constant source of inspiration and encouragement and who helped me at every step to solve my eternal problems of restlessness and lack of sublimated thoughts), Mr Arani Sen and Mr Indrayudh (a constant support), Professor Dr Shamik Ghosh (for his help as my host during my Calcutta field work), Ms Upama Dey (for being my hostess on many occasions during my field trips in Calcutta), Mr Maharshi Dey, Dr Eduardo de Castro (my host in Portugal and sincere friend), Ms. Helia de Castro (my hostess in Portugal and a mental support), Dr Joao Lourenco Marques and his family (my hosts in Portugal and sincere friends), Professor Dr Tapabrata Maiti and his family, especially Ms Titun Roy Maity, Miss Ovia Maity and Ms Indira Roy (our fabulous hosts and supporters during our regular stays in the US), Dr Sean Holly (our host during our stays in Cambridge), Dr Chris Higson, Dr Sushmita Maitra (my hostess in

Durham and sincere friend), Ms Paromita Bhattacharya and Professor Dr Subhamay Bhattachrya (my hosts and support in London), Mr Piyush Roy and Mr Pankaj Singh (for being a constant source of entertainment and wit in person and as a resource for films), Professor Dr Bashabi Fraser, Dr Bimalendu Bhattacharya and Dr Neil Fraser (for being my hosts in Edinburgh and a great support), Professor Dr Parantap Basu (my host in Durham and a sincere friend), Dr Rosen Azad Chowdhury and his family (for being my hosts on many occasions in the UK and Bangladesh), Professor Dr Monojit Chatterjee and Ms Anjum Rahamatullah (for being my hosts in Scotland and providing mental support), Mr Jonah Magar (my wonderful technical editor, for his immense patience), Mr Philipp Fritz (for kindly translating my thesis summary from English to German) and my comrades from the Socialist Workers Party (UK). I thank Mr Deep Purakayashtha for being my support and encouraging me to write this book. I thank Ms Rituparna Sen Gupta for being my real friend and sibling when I was in deep crisis and sustaining me in my madness. I thank Dr Shakuntala Chakraborty and my aunt Mrs Ela Sen for being my nice hostesses. Ms Bipasha Sen Roy was always there for me to carry out my madness. In a later period I received immense support and encouragement from Dr Subhayu Banerjee, Ms Pronita Banerjee and those two lovely gentlemen, Agnijo and Aryan. Mr Tapas Banerjee and Ms Sucharita Banerjee always helped me to recover from my depressions. I acknowledge Dr Anne Hamilton for helping me in editing this huge vulnerable book to a stronger one. I acknowledge Ritzy Rajaswi, Anindita, Anusuya, Sukanya, Saoni, Subhojit, Soumya, Paromita Hazra and all my friends from India and Edinburgh.

I remain indebted to Dr Anne Hamilton, my Story Shop 2016 friend, for her sincere help and support for almost a year in copyediting the text. She tolerated my idiosyncrasies and sustained my spirit by encouraging me at every step.

I acknowledge the libraries of Goethe University, University of St Andrews, University of Dundee and Heriot-Watt University, Michigan State University Main Library and the Mathematics Library and University of Edinburgh and staffs from the cafés.

I would also like to express my appreciation to Dr Dhrubajyoti Ghosh, who has died recently. He was one of my significant research teachers and a pioneer engineer of Wetland Conservation in Calcutta – one of the biggest projects in the world.

I am also extremely grateful to Dr Anne Hamilton, creative writing teacher from Edinburgh, who very carefully read the manuscript and at the same time taken care of the tenses and stresses of the book, and to my Story Shop 2016 friends (Edinburgh City of Literature) from Edinburgh International Book Festival.

This book would not have been completed, or even begun, without all your support, help and encouragement. I do not know how to thank you all enough.

Edinburgh
October 2017

1 Introduction

How is the socio-cultural and entrepreneurial space of the community of waste pickers in Calcutta created? One answer lies in the poem *Envoi* by Mexican poet Octavio Paz, the link of which is provided at the end of the chapter as the endnote.[1] It denotes the marginalised space which the neglected community shape and here they invest their socio-cultural and entrepreneurial activities during a finite period of history.

Introduction

This story of *Urban Marginalisation in South Asia: Waste Pickers in Calcutta* starts its journey with an urban community of waste pickers in Calcutta, India. It examines the life and society of a community that resides within the city while being on the periphery of mainstream society. Taking refuge in a no-man's land, this community nurtures its unique profession of transforming renewable waste into new resources for future use. The waste pickers convert this no-man's waste land of garbage into a living land: by nurturing their memories (both critically negative and positive), cultivating the idea of a new life (comprising enterprise and invention, negotiation, cynicism, pessimism and illusions) and fostering desires for escape. This strange world stands on its own against a hostile outside comprising the state, elites and mainstream society. Its residents continuously try to escape the 'ideal' uniform homogenous world: the legal professions; the shelter and sanitation; education and healthcare; savings and credit schemes and the cultural activities of the mainstream. The waste pickers are the pessimists who constantly attempt to deny the protection of 'normal behaviour' by the state, and accept the punishment of isolation and marginalisation due to their 'errant behaviour' in the eyes of the outside world.

However, since the community chooses to live outside the domain of main resources, it replaces this with an informal resource circuit that enables it to prosper economically by allowing the application of their visionary skills to choose the right trash and convert it into a valuable resource – thus earning more money. These days, the waste picker community is earning even more than many cross-sections of mainstream society. The people of the community can buy their daily necessities, and while the quality of the everyday goods they consume may be very low, they can survive more easily than before. Despite this improvement, though, they do not consider revising their position; they choose to remain outside the domain of mainstream/ elite society and the state. Money and financial resources do not work for them. As such, the waste pickers overcome their economic poverty but enter another trap of intense socio-cultural and religious marginalisation.

In choosing to remain at an arm's length distance from the state and mainstream society, the waste picker community has realised the immense benefits of their informal setting. Their reclusive social position provides them with the scope to escape from the authority of the state, even while 'stealing' the rubbish which is the state's property. The people of the community are both clever and visionary in understanding the huge value of recyclable waste. This garbage is almost neglected by the state, which does not understand the value of segregating general waste, and so does not even try to protect the environment by recycling properly. The reason behind the state's neglect of this segregation process is the significant financial cost incurred from their end. This is the gap filled in by the waste pickers; indeed, it is their only means of sustenance. And if this community understands one thing, it is the essence of survival. First, for this work they do not have to invest any money nor learn many skills. Second, if they move out of their marginalised position, they will lose the huge economic benefit gained by selling the stolen rubbish to the retailers. Simply, the waste pickers tolerate their marginal position to gain in the long run. They can evade and avoid state exploitation, taxation and stress related to a formal existence (Scott 2009) and they retain their freedom. In turn, the mainstream/ elite society and the state have the confidence and arrogance to feel they neither need the help of the marginalised community in any major activities, nor will they share their resources with them. Hence, they position the community outside their own periphery. Thus, from both sides the cycle of marginalisation is vicious, and it works on several levels: economic, social, religious and ritualistic, and cultural. This will be explained in detail in Chapter 2.

Economic marginalisation

The studied community has a long history. Since the 1930s, there has been a steady stream of migrants coming into Calcutta in search of jobs. They originate from rural parts of West Bengal, north and east India, and people displaced from Bangladesh. The waste picker community highlighted here constitutes a particularly disadvantaged segment of such economic migrants. After migrating, these people (predominantly Muslim) have taken up residence beside the railway tracks and heavily polluted canals in the eastern fringe areas of Calcutta: Park Circus, Tangra, Topsia and Tiljala. The specific history and geography of these areas characterise the nature of the socio-economic marginalisation of the community in residence. Covering the largest dumping and land filling sites around Calcutta, and the largest concentration of informal recycling units, the areas are not designated for human habitation. Squatter settlements (made of unhygienic plastic and jute material), food without adequate nutritional value, contaminated water and non-existent sewage facilities paint a grim picture of the urban marginalisation and poverty of this community. The residents have no permanent address or ration cards. Can these places be considered 'inaccessible', 'uncivilised and barbaric' (Scott 2009: 336)? Does the state find it difficult to install an effective sovereignty over these people (Scott 2009) who have no formal allegiance to formal state institutions?

Against the constraints of rising unemployment and exclusion from mainstream society, this community chooses the non-formal occupation of collecting recyclable material (different kinds of plastic, rubber, paper, glass, wood and some metals like iron and aluminium) and selling them to recycling units – an economic activity that receives no formal acknowledgement.[2] Those carrying out such work are exploited by their employers and by the state, and their earnings remain within the underground/ black economy. This story of their lives and community will attempt to answer the following questions: how do elite strategies contribute to control over power and resources, and thereby marginalisation? What factors induce people from different backgrounds to accept the history and reality of deprivation in these areas, and choose an occupation that contributes to economic marginalisation?

Socio-cultural marginalisation

Since their occupation involves handling waste products, the waste pickers are colloquially referred to as scavengers, and thus they remain untouchables outside the mainstream Muslim society of Calcutta. They are also abused by the police and mainstream civil society, and are called anti-social, untrustworthy, unreliable, immoral and shameless. Their important contribution to urban society is recognised by neither the state nor mainstream society. One of my key questions, then, is: how far do the waste pickers compromise with, or resist against, such social labels, and what can we learn about marginalisation from their role in the negotiation process?

Religious and ritualistic marginalisation is rife within this predominantly Muslim community. Although the individuals share elements of a broader faith in Islam, they seldom have allegiance to the formal religious establishments. During religious festivals, they are rarely invited for prayers or to share food and clothes. They do not participate in the ritualistic sacrifice of animals – a central part of the Eid and Bakhr-Eid festivals – and neither do they receive any share of the meat. Do their constraints with regard to time, space and resources lead them to withdraw from the mainstream religious and cultural authority? In general terms, marriage alliances are impossible between this community and other social and economic clans; the waste pickers are treated as outcasts even by other groups with more mainstream occupations but with similar subsistence patterns. Are they considered as polluting factors in marriage, burial and funeral rituals by mainstream society? Are they allowed to be buried in the same burial grounds? What are the taboos relating to their marriage alliances and burial and funeral activities within their own societies and neighbourhoods and beyond? I will tell the tales of their marriages, their loves, their betrayals and their rituals relating to birth and to burials and funerals.

Cultural marginalisation is insidious since most of the waste picker community is either illiterate or, at best, non-formally educated. Since so few people have attended formal schools or madrasas, they cannot actively participate in any reading sessions, including those of religious texts. They are mostly forbidden from the cultural functions of mainstream society, partly because of taboos relating to their inferior dietary and 'unhealthy' occupational practices. However, if resources are available, the community try to organise their own cultural programmes during marriages and other social events. In this way, the cultural practices of the community can be considered as a strategy to avoid indignity, insult and injury from mainstream society. In my research, I attempt to solve the puzzle of how the migrant marginalised people from different places accept and internalise the history and culture of this area.

Rationale

To date, the life and society of the waste pickers of Calcutta and their experience of marginalisation is a vastly under-researched area. My work is inspired and informed by limited information about the community available from two previous, non-academic studies, Bhattacharya and Sen (1997) and Sen and Islam (2000). These studies are grounded in rudimentary information that I collected while working within the community as a social researcher and social worker for the NGO Tiljala Society for Human and Educational Development (T-SHED) during the period 1994–2003. While that research was not ethnographic, but based on ad-hoc surveys, primarily the completion of questionnaires, the data is a starting point for insights both into the socio-economic, cultural and religious-ritualistic marginalisation of the subject population, and for exploring research gaps and questions regarding their marginalisation. The focal point of this previous work was exploring the visionary behaviour of the waste pickers in terms of their informal occupation (collection and segregation of waste) and acknowledging their lack of due recognition for it. At that time, the community did not participate in any socio-cultural or religious programmes and were rarely invited to any feasts organised by retailers. When I started my social work in 1996, and resumed as a social researcher in 2003, the community was, in addition to their socio-cultural and religious marginalisation, economically poor; they lacked capacity to purchase necessities. As such, their economic poverty influenced their social and cultural marginalisation.

During this current fieldwork (ethnography over the period 2011–13), I discovered that the community has developed economically. By Indian standards, these waste pickers are no longer living under the poverty line; yet they remain significantly marginalised in social, religious and cultural (ideological) terms. It is this observation that forms the fundamental motivation for my present work. The research outputs that constitute this book comprise general and specific characterisation and different dimensions of marginalisation in terms of the community, and document the kind of recognition about the community's contribution towards their own and mainstream society. These outputs are hereby disseminated not only to the academic research community, but also to policymakers, public officials, private-sector operators and NGOs involved with the conservancy field (including both formal and informal waste management systems).

Research methodology

Throughout, I employ interpretive ethnography of the studied community, focusing on ideological and cultural marginalisation, as distinct from economic marginalisation, to examine the waste picker community and a world that is virtually unknown to outsiders. Over two phases of ethnographical fieldwork (2011–13), I have utilised participant observation and personal interviews as my main methodologies. This leads to cataloguing the processes which build up the story of marginalisation, and subsequently connecting it with existing literature on marginalisation. It is essential to recognise that the data gathering, and its analysis, contain an interpretative process from my (the researcher's) end, and that early data analysis provides sufficient insight to plan the gathering of further data.

The first phase of my field work began in October 2011 and lasted until December 2011. The exact location of this population is in ward numbers of 58, 59 and 66 of Calcutta Municipal Corporation. Ward number 58 in the north is bounded by a sewage outlet where it meets with New Canal; in the south it is bounded by Tangra Road and the southern embankment of the storm water outlet where it meets with the New Canal. In the east, this settlement is bounded by Topsia Road and the New Canal and in the west by the Eastern Railway. Ward number 59 is bounded in the north by Christopher Road, south by Topsia Road, Tiljala Road and Gorachand Road. The east is bounded by Gobindo Chandra Khatick Road and Topsia Road (south) and the west is bounded by Topisa Road (south), Tiljala Road and Dr Sundari Mohan Avenue. This squatter settlement is also covered by ward number 66, Topsia Road (south and north) in the north; Picnic Garden Road in the south; Pashchim Chowbagha in the east and Tiljala Road, Kustia Road, Gobindo Chandra Khatick Road and Topsia Road in the west.

The second phase of field work, at the Park Circus squatter settlement, ran from December 2012 to March 2013. This settlement is only few yards away from my own home at Gobra Kabarsthan and just beside the Eastern Railway lines. The exact location of the field is in ward number 35 (Municipality Calcutta). It is bounded in the north by Eastern Railway, in the south by Abinash Seshmal Lane, in the east by Raja Rajendralal Mitra Road and in the west by Eastern Railway.

The first period of study comprised entering the field – a straightforward (though never easy) task, given my earlier career as the social researcher for an NGO with a strong field base inside the community. The field staff of this NGO introduced me formally to community leaders and the elders. The club members recognised me very quickly. Thus, despite the eight years since my first work, I received a very friendly welcome, and the community shared its views and opinions without hesitation. Being a native of Calcutta, I faced no problems with language, conversing easily in Bengali, Hindi and Urdu, and my long-term experience of the community's views and position was extremely helpful. Through intensive field work (participant observation, interviews and focus group discussions) I strengthened my knowledge of the waste pickers' history, politics and economics, and their culture, as such identifying the changes, and the nature of intervention, which the community people have undergone in recent years. Of note was my ability – with the help of the club members – to gain entrance to an informal gambling den inside the community settlement. It took 15 days of silence, demonstrating my skill at card games, and proving I would not disturb their gambling, or gossip about it outside, for the members to trust me.

Sometimes such rapport between researcher and subject could make the situation complex. On one hand, I used my contacts and experience to become an 'insider', on the other, I deliberately maintained a distance to collect unbiased data. Ultimately it worked: an essential balance for a research topic that was apparently simple but contested social boundaries, including such sensitive issues as religious and cultural beliefs, their love life and their sexual behaviours. From the outset, my main concern was gaining access to suitable participants, to engage them in qualitative research and not to do any harm; always, my work had to be ethically sound and protect people's psychological, physical and/or professional welfare. I won the confidence of the main gatekeepers of the fields by taking time to establish relationships, bonding with families through prolonged engagement. My participant observation concentrated on two families, and reciprocity and mutual obligation was very important, especially with the children. Rapport-building was a crucial factor in receiving the insider status that permitted me to listen in to conversations and watch activities and behaviours within family lives. Thus, gaining such trust to enter the field was straightforward but not easy. It required constant negotiation with all parties: the local club secretary and club members, with NGO staff, with community individuals and families. For my part, I tried to be non-judgemental as far as possible, and was tested. For example, when I heard that women still give birth in their squatter settlement I was shocked, imagining that both mother and child could so easily die in such unhygienic conditions. I had to rationalise it: as their reality, which is very different to mine, and I could recognise their perspective. The waste picker community does not receive humane treatment from state hospitals and health care systems and the medical facilities are out of their reach. Hence, they prefer giving birth in their community settlement, or they simply neglect their medical treatments. Thus, I could set my judgements aside.

The subsequent participant observation and interviewing has allowed my research multiple layers and perceptions of realities. It has generated so many behavioural patterns, stories, gossip and rumours which helped to formulate my analysis of the community's socio-cultural and religious domains, their relationships, and to identify their fears, abstentions, very few aspirations and dreams. The overall field work has granted me a holistic view of the community's behaviour that characterises them, and the ethnography has given me the lens to see through their interrelationships.

My research data consists of recorded observation and interviews in the form of field notes. I have reports on the experiences of, and interviews with, various stakeholders. The field notes were taken mainly by hand, and within a short period entered into a computer. First, I collected their words, their stories, in short incomplete sentences, then these interactions were transformed into full-scale descriptions with quotations following my return home, barely a mile away. I also took photographs of the community people and their life. Those featured in the accompanying pictures not only gave their permission to be photographed, but were very keen to pose. I was unable to use more sophisticated instruments such as tape recorder/voice recorder because the community people did not like the concept of recording their voices, and as such it would have been unethical. I believe that such restrictions have given my research more spontaneous and honest viewpoints. I spent nine hours (9 a.m. to 6 p.m.) in the field throughout two three-month phases. These long hours helped the participant observation to avoid biases associated with researcher perspective – of legal and illegal matters, formal and non-formal issues in terms of profession, market, roads, private and public spaces, exploitation or being distanced from the state and mainstream/elite society, schools and health care. These long hours on a daily basis, together with my existing knowledge of the field, brought about trust, and produced compelling stories woven with the waste pickers' voices and experiences. These material observations give actual evidence to the thesis ethnography which portray truthfully the waste pickers' repressed or denied life existence as opposed to any 'ideal' behaviour; for example, participating in any social/cultural projects organised by the NGOs. The research illustrates how families, social organisations and their cultural aspects (like Bollywood and Hindi songs and dances) respond to their environmental conditions and leave both physical and psychological traces.

The final point in the methodology is about self-knowledge. I have tried to mix my own personal experiences with the community's shared and lived experiences. In the initial phase, I worried that the 'wrong' data was collected, or that I had huge gaps in it. The second phase of fieldwork was an opportunity to learn, reflect and deal with any points left undone in the first phase. The fieldwork itself has created a strong impact upon my outlook and future intentions. It has, undoubtedly, transformed my personality by developing more patience and exploratory potentials. I have become more adaptable to new values and feel a strong ethical commitment towards the community. For example, when between 400 and 450 of the waste picker community's shelters were gutted by fire in April 2014, I felt a strong desire to, literally, stand beside the people. However, I understood that my supportive role was to continue to tell their stories, and detail the fire and the continuum of their lives. I was also able to collect and donate money for their well-being after this calamity. (This is also a practical example of ethics when dealing with sensitive issues. The challenge of asking community members about tragic experiences was duly recognised throughout. At all times, the privacy and the value of the time of the community, and of other stakeholders, was fully respected.)

Structure of the book

Having now set the scene for my research, the remainder of this book both analyses my findings and then goes on to explore the current research gaps of ideological marginalisation in the waste picker community. Given the multiplicity of views on marginality and marginalisation, I will address many questions in respect of the community. First, what are the specific resource imbalances, ideological changes and altered subsistence potentials of the marginalised researched community that serve to make them marginal? Second, what, if any, are the non-stratified and non-formal processes which the marginalised community adopt for their subsistence? Third, is the community persistently ostracised and excluded from mainstream social life? And what, if any, are their socio-economic, cultural and religious obligations to, and exchanges with, mainstream society? Finally, which of the dimensions – spatial (shelter location and pattern), economic (class, income and food intake), social (social labelling, food pattern and social events), cultural (ethnicity, education, myth, taboos, symbols and cultural events) and religious (prayer, festivals and ritualistic practices within marriage, funerals and related food patterns) – characterise the marginality of the waste picking community? Overall, the social justice, or politics, of stigmatisation, marginalisation and humiliation in general, and the specific communities of waste pickers in their everyday live, are central to this book, and the chapters are structured accordingly. As a starting point, it seeks to evaluate the extent to which the government/state, elites and mainstream society are engaged in discussions about the community's problems in public discourses, as well as any efforts made to address their problems and intentions to resolve these through social welfare schemes. Subsequent chapters analyse the decisions and participation of the waste pickers in such processes of negotiation, considering their relatively detached position in relation to mainstream life. Further, it examines their situation by describing the community's conflicting habits and the trust, or lack thereof, that they place in the outside world. Emphasis is placed on the public discourses that, with certainty and subtlety, devalue the position of the community. These are understood via different theories that explain the community's position through comparison with other similarly situated communities.

Chapter 2 (Literature and theoretical framework) studies the main foundations and cultures of inequality, focusing on learned theoretical frameworks. It develops a synthesis of extant contributions in social anthropology and other scholarly works examining marginalisation. In doing so, it addresses the complexities through which general marginalisation is linked to socio-cultural and ritualistic marginalisation (referred to from hereon in as ideological marginalisation) in relation to under-privileged groups in both urban and agricultural societies. In Chapter 3 (Ideological marginalisation versus economic marginalisation) the realities of urban desolation and the social despair of the community are captured. There is a focus on the link between ideological and economic marginalisation and, more precisely, the need is raised to examine, theoretically and ethnographically, the connections between urban desolation and socio-cultural denigration within the waste picker community. It emphasises 'how the daily material experience of material dilapidation, seclusion, and socio-cultural-economic marginality translates into the corrosion of the self, rasping of interpersonal ties, and skewing of public policies through the mediation of sulphurous cognition fastened onto a defamed place' (Wacquant 2010a). Thus Chapter 3 addresses both the crisis (depreciation) and strength of ideological marginalisation. It covers the collective depreciation of the waste picking community's social and material resources and the reasons behind their chronic depression. It addresses how waste pickers negotiate with those who consider their community as 'destitute and dispirited' (Wacquant 2010a). Despite this hegemonic and axiomatic consideration by the outside world, the waste pickers are determined to continue their unique business, with its distinctive ambience, in such a hostile milieu. The chapter describes how this is possible, as the community is aware of its own 'moral degradation', and knows that this degradation is not the cause of their deep crisis and problems.

Chapter 4 (Silent defence and subtle negotiation) points out the gap in the study of ideological marginalisation in terms of negotiation between marginalised people and all other stake holders. An attempt to fill this gap follows by demonstrating how the waste picker community, through their selective participation and non-participation in their profession and other activities of education, healthcare and training projects, negotiate with different strata of the hierarchy. Together, Chapters 3 and 4 examine how, even after the waste pickers' repeated attempts at negotiation with the hierarchy, the mainstream state policies shift away from supporting these residents at the fringes. Through local institutions, the public services leave this community experiencing joblessness, poverty and escalating crime, with an informal life orientation. However, the community has developed an alternative economy, social relations and cultural aspects to fill the vacuum left by the formal economy. This is followed further in Chapter 5 (Challenging social capital: Formulation and/or subversion), which focuses on the symbolic denigration and entrapment of the waste picker community at the bottom of the hierarchy of spaces within the city of Calcutta. The community's feelings of dejection, depression and utter cynicism are manifestations of different aspects of ideological marginalisation. These are analysed through attention to the theories of socio-cultural and human capitals of Bourdieu (1983), Coleman (1988), and Putnam (1995, 2000). In combination with the community's everyday life, these theories reveal that the alienation of its objective life chances, in turn, collapses the social horizon of subjective expectations, leaving little room between utter despair and their pessimistic dreams.

There is a shift of emphasis in Chapter 6 (Kinship and neighbourhood: Life without husbands and fathers) with an exploration of kinship among the waste pickers, concentrating on the effect of absent male figures. Information is drawn from sole mother–daughter units and the position of the waste pickers within the community's social, cultural and ritualistic processes (related to birth, marriage, everyday challenges in household and neighbourhood life, and death and funerals) through the theories of socio-cultural capital (Bourdieu 1983, 1986; Coleman 1988), human capital and bridging (which helps a community to advance in every aspect of economics, socio-cultural life) and bonding (inward-looking, connecting homogenous people) of social capital of Putnam (1995, 2000). These processes clearly demonstrate that the community lacks a 'good stock of social capital' (Putnam 2000) in which their individual connections arise only through social bonding, instead of their 'social networks', 'norms of reciprocity' and 'trustworthiness'. In their kinship, the waste pickers can rarely depend on social resources and social capital to draw upon in times of crisis.

At this point, we can summarise as to why the waste pickers of Calcutta, the little-known community described in this book, is interesting and important. What are the significant qualities of this community that demand a book-length treatment focusing on their socio-cultural marginalisation in their everyday life? The book will show how this apparently 'hopeless, chaotic and flop' community, as it has been described by the conservancy sector's mayor in council (Calcutta), state police, elites and mainstream society, is dramatically innovative and entrepreneurial. While some factors appear to show this community to be tremendously non-cohesive and problematic, its members have their own routine structure and reproduce their own habits generation after generation. For example, every day without fail, the waste pickers go out between 2 and 4 a.m. in search of recyclable waste to contribute to the process of recycling and, unknowingly, to the conservation of the environment without state help or mainstream/elite support. In concentrating on two illegal waste pickers' settlements in the Indian city of Calcutta, exploring different stories and the multiple layers of marginalisation of the waste pickers' community, this book dissects marginalisation in general. It examines whether economic marginalisation (inequality in terms of material resources) has the greater strength to influence this waste picking community's ideological marginalisation (the community's social and cultural and ritualistic marginalisation), or whether their ideological marginalisation depreciates their social and human capital, which in turn prevents the waste pickers from going ahead with their plan to make a business of waste. This prohibition from carrying out their business arises from the community's entirely informal/non-formal existence on the fringes of the big city of Calcutta.

I prefaced this introduction with Octavio Paz's poem *Envoi*, words that symbolise the space created and maintained by the waste pickers of Calcutta. This is a space that not only forms the person's surrender to and acceptance of the injustices of the world, but also becomes that person's refuge, where s/he finds solace. This space denotes her/his working space, living space and her/his ultimate creative and leisure space. This space (the abstract space in Paz's concept), although excluded from the Calcutta city planners' matrix of urban design, can provide alternative characteristics with a minimal mainstream/state presence, evoking a different modern-day space for the waste pickers. This community represents more than one culture, time and place. Hence, this community creates its own space where its members fit best, a space often misunderstood and distorted by others like the state and the mainstream/elites. It is my intention to explore such 'spaces'.

Notes

1 Octavio Paz's poem *Envoi* describes symbolically how the waste picker community would have innovated their space with imagination, socio-cultural and entrepreneurial skills and resistance against their marginalisation and neglect. The poem is reproduced in Henri Lefebvre's *The Production of Space*; see, for example, https://dickiewebb.wordpress.com/2012/10/09/octavio-paz/.

2 Further, they are engaged in illegitimate work. Since such waste (from businesses, markets, hotels and restaurants, industries and factories, as well as domestic waste) is, under Indian law, the property of the government, their work with rubbish is essentially illegal and classified as theft.

2 Literature and theoretical framework

Fully understanding the marginalised position of the waste pickers of Calcutta, requires, first and foremost, definition and deconstruction of the concept of marginalisation itself, and in all its relevant forms. Thus, I begin by concentrating on ideological marginalisation, starting with its history and theoretical background before going on to debate ideological marginalisation versus economic marginalisation. Throughout this chapter there are references to a number of key anthropological theories, mainly by Appadurai (1996a, 1996b, 2006a, 2006b), Arnold (1993, 1995a, 1995b), Bourdieu (1991), Holston (1989, 1995, 1998, 2008, 2009), Scott (1985, 2009) and Wacquant (2007a, 2008, 2010a). These comparative theories[1] point to the need to elaborate, theoretically and ethnographically, on the connections between the ideological and the socio-economic marginalisation happening in peripheral cores vis-à-vis the more visible, apparently transparent, state, mainstream and elite society. As such, they strongly underpin my own ethnographic findings. My subsequent discussion highlights how the state and elites (or mainstream society) justify and negotiate marginalisation; how the marginalised – in this case, the waste pickers – classify their own marginalisation; how different voices and dimensions of marginalisation work and how are they related.

Ideological marginalisation

Ideological marginalisation refers to the exclusion of thus marginalised communities in dimensions that go far beyond the constraints of inadequate food, poor living conditions and low income. It concerns the perception (from either the ostracised group's or the mainstream/elite/state's point of view) of a lack of socio-cultural, economic, and religious and ritualistic participation, with an impact on the marginalised community's obligations and exchanges. The closer to one another the agents, groups or institutions are situated within the contextual space, the more common properties they have; the more distant they are, the fewer they have (Bourdieu 1989). For marginalised people like the waste pickers, exchanges with, and obligations to, the state and the mainstream/elite society are rare. Waste pickers are reluctant to share any common practices with their 'opposition', as all respective parties see their own positions as distant from the others. Spatial segregation leads to the phenomenon whereby state and the waste pickers who are remote from each other in social space tend to find themselves – by choice or necessity – distant from one another in geographic space. Nevertheless, while waste pickers and the state are very distant in social space, they can 'encounter one another and interact briefly and intermittently in physical space' (Bourdieu 1989: 16).

Clearly, the waste picker community is a case in point. While within the Calcutta city boundaries, it is limited to a squatter enclave situated on peripheral land, with minimal exchange or obligations between it and wider society – interaction is largely at the behest of the state when it wishes to avail itself of the services that the waste pickers can provide. The state/mainstream/elites justify such segregation by stating that they and these marginalised people have very few common properties and practices (Bourdieu 1989); hence, beyond official communications there is little value in interaction. This leads to the waste pickers being unable to acquire personal and social membership of the mainstream – and as Bourdieu (1989) would have it, this can be extended to any community denied access to any family, kinship community, club or any other solidarity group where access is refused – and ideological marginalisation is thus unavoidable. This also happens when marginal people are not sufficiently socially connected to procure 'legally recognised jobs, valuable information and investment opportunities' (Bourdieu 1989: 278). The waste pickers, for instance, cannot sustain these social and cultural connections, as they are not allowed to conduct the 'exchange of both material and symbolic goods, for example, gifts and mutual recognition' with members of the elite/mainstream society. This book argues that when the waste pickers cannot build up a social network then they are inevitably excluded from 'material and symbolic resource centre(s)' (Bourdieu 1989: 278). It is clear from my ethnography (2011–13) that this is exactly what has happened in this waste picker community.

Theories of marginalisation

The traditional view within anthropology (Cerulli 1922; Huntingford 1931; Straube 1963) is to understand marginalised people within a framework of ethnicity, caste or class. However, Cerulli (1930) and Haberland (1962) conclude that marginalised people may not have had a common ethnic origin. The waste pickers are unified by a common pattern of discrimination and taking refuge in a specialised craftwork or occupation. Further, myths and taboos, especially dietary distinctions or unwanted polluting occupations, are common denominators for categorising marginalisation (Braukämper 1984; Haberland 1979). The waste pickers are victims within both arguments. They are overwhelmingly Muslim, but are relegated to the periphery even within wider Islamic society, and general society, because of their ghettoisation and the untouchable nature of their profession.

As such, emerging mainstream society and accompanying elites fundamentally drive this process of marginalisation to promote their own advancement in socio-economic terms (Arnold 1993, 1995a, 1995b; Kelly 1991). The waste pickers' marginalisation revolves around elite/mainstream society strategies to develop control over power and other resources, creating resource imbalances and altering the subsistence potentials of populations like theirs. Such social differentiation through non-stratified and non-formal processes is related to power and politics that are dependent on human agency (Arnold 1995a). In essence, rule makers will tacitly accept the work carried out by the waste pickers because it suits them: nobody in mainstream society wants to be involved in waste collection and recycling but it has to be done, so 'allowing' a willing marginalised group to do it solves the problem. Certainly, I have found that some consultation and negotiation will be required between the waste pickers and the mainstream society (NGOs, corporate sector and Government Conservancy section) and state but this communication is in any case an essential part of the success of mainstream society/elite in the emergence of social hierarchy (Binford 1983; Brumfiel 1992; Paynter 1985). Relations between the mainstream majority and the marginalised minority (waste pickers) are not categorically ones of exploitation of one group by the other, but rather are based on individual 'patron–subordinate' relations (Amborn 1990: 398). This need for not only economic, but also social, cultural and religious exclusion between the mainstream and marginalised societies generates a continuous structured interaction, which may negate the image of total exclusion and segregation of the marginalised people (Pankhurst 2003).

The term marginalisation is used to focus attention on vital socio-economic changes and processes that accompany socio-cultural inequality in a range of social and cultural contexts – and the waste pickers of Calcutta are, again, a very specific example. Marginalising behaviour can happen at different nodes of social interaction and in societies of various scales (Arnold 1993, 1995a, 1995b). It begins inside households and communities themselves; indeed, it is rife within the waste picker community, and my ethnography complements that of Meillassoux (1981), who rests his argument on social controls, for example, on the control of elders over marriages, with a political motivation; he largely ignores the impact of both technological discoveries and mainstream/elite ambitions. Beyond that, marginalising behaviour is also prevalent in societies of any type or size at borders and frontiers, as well as between elites/mainstream society and marginalised people – wherein the people who are becoming elites in the mainstream society (like the NGO personnel) plan socio-economic changes of the waste pickers and clearly contest positions that are beyond their control.

The process of marginalisation involves elite strategies asserting control over labour, culture, politics, resources and information (Arnold 1993; Brumfiel 1992; Gosden 1989; Hayden 1995), which in turn creates dependencies, obligations and debts among the marginalised waste pickers. The ability of aspiring elites/mainstream leaders to negotiate with the waste pickers in terms of their labour, transportation, crafts/occupation, information and resources gives a clue to their own success in terms of building up their power and thus giving birth to dependencies of the non-elites. The reality of the social positioning of the two groups – the mounting power of elites/mainstream society and created dependencies of the marginalised/non-elite cluster of waste pickers – shows the unambiguous exploitation involved.

My research supports the notion that consultation and negotiation with those 'who are being marginalised is an essential part of elite/mainstream society/employers/patrons' success in the emergence of social hierarchy' Brumfiel (1992). While the process of marginalisation does engender increasing power inequalities as the elites/mainstream society take charge of the contexts in which they will work, the waste pickers can also participate by resisting the hegemony. They give their opinions in terms of their 'rewards and benefits, whether they be ideological or material', and in broader terms they can resist or cooperate with hierarchisation or newly imposed ideologies (Brumfiel 1992; Paynter 1985; Pankhurst 1999, 2003). Focusing on the perspectives of the waste pickers themselves seeks to 'understand ways in which the marginalised, while excluded from certain activities, could simultaneously be included as significant actors in the social and cultural reproduction of society'. Negative terms like 'depressed', 'submerged' and 'pariah' (outcast) and the image of complete ostracism portray a complex reality of simultaneous integration and exclusion of marginalised people (Amborn 1990: 409). To put it explicitly, from the mainstream point of view, waste pickers are a necessary evil – and as such, they are not entirely powerless; the evidence lies in the fact that they do survive as a community, and with a specific lifestyle. However, I would contend that such marginalisation partially (at least) arises from a passive process: when the population increases many more are unfortunately forced to take up certain occupations and thus fall to a lower echelon (Arnold 1995a: 94). This actually has little to do with direct mainstream/elite manipulation, meaning that on some level, the marginalised waste pickers are simply victims. From this perspective, the rise of social differentiation is unrelated to 'ambition, power, or politics; there is no role for human agency, socioeconomic negotiation, factional competition' (Arnold 1995a: 94).

Analysing marginalisation from five interrelated dimensions – spatial, economic, political, social and cultural – it is a fact, then, that minorities are not always marginalised in the same way or for the same reasons; often it is a combination of circumstances. It can be considered as a power relation between the dominant (the state/mainstream/elites) and the dominated or marginalised (Bourdieu 1989). This power relation creates a pole within the field of power. There is a symmetric and inverse order of power between the dominant and the dominated according to their economic or cultural capitals in terms of politics, civil services and their professions. The fundamental powers are economic capital (in its different forms), cultural capital, social capital and symbolic capital, which are the forms that the various species of capital assume when they are perceived and recognised as legitimate (Bourdieu 1986a). Thus, resources are distributed in the overall social space and among different agents according to the overall volume of legitimate capitals they possess and according to the structure of their assets (Bourdieu 1989).

It is important to point out that against these legitimate capitals, different forms of non-formal capitals have entered the arena of the marginalised waste pickers as they seek to evade domination by the formal capitals. While holders of the various capitals compete, marginalised communities create their own non-formal capitals and spaces through their own economic and cultural activities – such as taking up waste picking as their profession to gain access to the non-formal and illegitimate economic capital. This takes place alongside activities such as gambling, addiction and watching cheap videos, copying Bollywood/Bengali films and television serials; the marginalised waste pickers of Calcutta still retain their rural songs and dances parallel to Bollywood culture as their own cultural capital. Further, in order to survive, they tap/hook electricity, create their own makeshift toilets and sanitation, and procure impure drinking water and polluted water for washing from the canal. They even create their own geographical spaces for transportation and their illegitimate businesses. My ethnography (2011–13) shows that the NGO management and staff, mainstream/elite and state in the whole structure of domination exert their power quite subtly through existing political, social and economic orders. Although the elites, state and other stake holders try to define the structure of social space and govern the life chances and trajectories of the community and individual waste pickers through their economic and cultural capital, it should be noted that the community also sets its own economic and cultural parameters and defines its own social spaces.

I examine how the mainstream society/elites describe the marginalised waste pickers as 'infirm, the religiously deviant, the mobile, the illegal, and unwelcome in the space of the nation-state marked as unhealthy, disloyal, needed but unwelcome because of their anomalous identities' (Appadurai 1996a), in order to show them as failures – and in my ethnography, who or what can be a greater failure than a transient waste picker in a squatter colony? The state and mainstream society/elites endeavour to represent them as victims who are 'sub-human, vermin, insects, scum, garbage, and yet a cancerous part of the valued national body so they can avoid them, deny them and eliminate them in a pessimistic vision to own them, control them and use them'. I would strongly argue that the waste pickers are the flashpoint for a series of uncertainties that mediate between everyday life and its fast-shifting global backdrop. This community creates uncertainties about national self and citizenship. Their legal status is quite ambiguous, which can destabilise the meanings of consumption and the legal system; their movements threaten the policing system; their monetary transactions almost never come under national economies and usually stand between legal and criminal transactions; their mixed and unsophisticated languages question national cultural coherence. Spending time within the waste picker community, I have experienced first-hand how their lifestyles constitute an easy way to create tensions in urban set ups, their lives being multi-focal and a source of anxiety to the security of the state. When some of them manage to create wealth, they become a sore point for elite economics, and when they are poor, they become convenient symbols of failure in the chain of development and welfare. This is reality for the waste pickers.

From this point of view, 'marginality began where sovereignty and tax ended' (Scott 2009: 31). Thus, waste picking people 'are best understood as runaway, fugitive, marooned communities – fleeing the oppressions of the state-making projects of slavery, conscription, taxes, forced labour, epidemics, and warfare' (Scott 2009: IX). The characteristics that stigmatise the waste pickers are their very location at the margins, their physical migration, their occupation and diet, their flexible social and kinship structures, their religious heterodoxy, their egalitarianism and their non-literate oral culture. These features of their economic, social and cultural life are better adapted to survival if they remain non-subjects in the political environment of states rather than making states themselves. Hence, they have invented their own culture and heterodox religion to evade hierarchical, codified 'state capture and state formation' (Scott 2009: 9). I can symbolically evaluate the self-governing (marginalised) people and the state-governed (mainstream) people respectively – 'variously styled as the raw and the cooked, the wild and the tamed, the barbarian and the civilized, the backward and the modern, without history and with history' which provide many possibilities for 'comparative triangulation' (Scott 2009: 3).

Ideological marginalisation versus economic marginalisation

It is possible to equate marginalisation with social inequality and in doing so to investigate the role of status differentiation in traditional anthropological and archaeological debates and major societal transitions (Arnold 1995a). This evaluates the process of marginalisation as a force in the rise and enforcement of socio-economic inequality in a range of societies, including complex urban societies, akin to the waste picking community. In this case, the definition of marginalisation is 'the process by which established or emerging elites create socio-economic relations of superior versus subordinate/dependent through manipulations of labour and distributions of social resources' (Arnold 1995a: 88). 'Rising elites' and mainstream society gather power, privilege and status and these elites also learn to control the information or technology (Kelly 1991) that is critically important to their economic success. Thus, orchestrating their network and limiting power within their own small circle, the mainstream society prevents the waste picking community from attaining positions with substantial political, cultural and economic resources. The impact of this process of marginalisation is permanent social inequality between elites/mainstream society and the waste pickers. Elite/mainstream power, here the retailers and recycling units' owners' power includes primarily control over waste pickers' labour and over information and transportation which leads to the mainstream society like the NGOs becoming the labour brokers for lineages and local-level activities and social interaction. In terms of the waste pickers, I believe this argument may well be indicative of their relationships with their retailers – the middle men – between them and the recycling units owners, and it is something I will return to at a later stage.

To summarise, the above discussion of relevant literature, and the way it provides a framework for my ethnography of the waste pickers of Calcutta, serves to demonstrate two distinctly different models of marginalisation. The first is the political, human agency model. This sees changes as driven by opportunism, ambition, active processes of social negotiation and the passive-inevitable model. In all cases, marginalisation involves isolating some people from positions of social and economic influence and resources, alienating them from major decision-making. This process leaves the isolated party dependent on the elites for their socio-economic, cultural and religious activities (Arnold 1995a). On the other hand, the second model emphasises the subtle and passive resistance of marginal people in order to survive independently and defend themselves (Scott 1985). Certainly, within the waste picker community, the usual weapons of resistance against their powerless state are: feigned ignorance, flight, theft, slander, arson, cultural resistance and the sabotage of any performance or programme. These processes represent a form of self-help and require little or no co-ordination, skill or planning. Their struggle mostly stops well short of collective outright defiance. Since this concept of 'quiet' resistance is at the core of the waste pickers' behaviours, I will discuss it in depth below.

Marginalisation in a developing country urban context

I will reiterate that the waste pickers of Calcutta, living in an urban fringe area, are clear examples of marginalisation in an urban context of a developing country. They are considered to be homeless, invariably to have migrated, and to have marginalised neighbourhoods. They construct their own shelters on the peripheries with precarious materials and illegitimate conditions, which are widely known as squatter settlements. They represent sites of insurgence as they introduce new identities and practices into the city that disturb established histories. Analysing their circumstances encourages us to explore 'spaces' in urban areas; touching upon different social imaginations and insurgent citizenship. These insurgent, or fringe, spaces may be described as the truth of modernism. Insurgency describes the new sources of spaces and practices that assert an opposition to the existent civil law and the concept that the state is the only legitimate source of citizenship rights, meanings and civil practices. This insurgency may lead to new forms of social structures, which are absorbed into the old and indicate uncertain alternative futures.

In modern life, it is apparent that modernist systems of traffic circulation reject insurgent street systems of public spaces. Modernist planners consider the latter too congested and unhealthy for the city population. The social consequence of this rejection is very clear. By eliminating these kinds of insurgent streets, the modern city planners in Calcutta eliminate a section of the urban population that was supported within it. Whether we label the waste pickers 'insurgent citizens', or 'marginalised communities', it remains that they are alienated from the streets and squares of the mainstream citizens, denied the indoor rooms of malls, clubs and car parking, and deprived of their fair share of outdoor public spaces. In response they create their own spaces. These no-man's lands – here, the waste pickers' squatter settlements – established, protected and utilised by the community itself, allow the marginalised groups to feel in control of some aspects of their lives and living. In this way, both they and the mainstream and elites build up their own respective areas that are completely forbidden to each other. And in turn, city planners, who are directed by conventional state dictums and neglectful of the issues of insurgent citizenship or non-citizens (Holston 2008, 2009), run the risk that the marginalised will parody, derail and subvert state and NGO agendas through their irregular educational, cultural and social activities. My ethnography (2011–13) demonstrates exactly how the waste picker community does this.

The waste pickers of Calcutta, like all marginalised people without dignity, are universally viewed with contempt. The mainstream opposition, without exception, looks at them as 'dispossessed households' and 'dishonoured minorities' (Wacquant 2008: 1). The state believes them to be the most sombre migrant community. I have documented the waste pickers' social life (and found it similar to that described and analysed by Arnold, Holston, Appadurai and Wacquant) as almost an exact replica of the model where the social life of the marginal 'appears to be barren, chaotic and brutish' (Wacquant 2008: 1) and the reason behind this wretched condition of marginalised people is frequently the incapacity of the relevant states. States refuse to 'check the social and spatial accumulation of economic hardship, social dissolution and cultural dishonour' (Wacquant 2008: 7) of the marginalised people, indirectly create 'chronic civic alienation' (Wacquant 2008: 7)' and provoke the non-participation of marginalised people, which, along with their alienation, poses a challenge to the institution of citizenship. In the urban context of the waste pickers, social disorders are tackled by the apparently tough state policies with the help of the police and law (Wacquant 2008: 7). However, this penalisation of the marginal by the state can only promote the darkness inside the life of these marginal people while state welfare breaks down for them. The state should keep in mind that marginalised people in the fringe areas should be made part of the urban planning (Appadurai 2006b; Appadurai and Holston 1999) and may 'move towards the institutionalization of a right to subsistence outside of the tutelage of the market' (Wacquant 2008: 7).

The waste pickers embody the argument that marginalised people flee from the state and make themselves exempt from state tax and other state formalities and regulations (Scott 2009). This way, they keep the state at a safe distance from them. In this respect, the degree and form of state intervention 'in the neighbourhoods of relegation' should be considered so that the waste pickers' relations with the different state and mainstream/elite apparatus, institutions and organisations can be measured. This will indicate how far they maintain their relations with the schools, hospitals, housing, transportation, public spaces and social welfare (Wacquant 2008). And, as I go on to describe in later chapters, the waste picker community is a consistently reluctant client of any such social services available to them, irrespective of whether the state or an NGO is the supplier. Still, these relationships between marginal people and the opposition cannot be assumed to be 'static, uniform, univocal' (Wacquant 2008: 11). Such relationships give birth to complaints and conflicts from both the opposition and marginal people. These complaints and conflicts open up a potential space for new meanings and multiple exchanges. A unique example of this interaction (or lack of) lies in the already-mentioned relationships between the waste pickers, the waste retailers and the opposition, and as already, again, promised, we will return to this later on.

Marginalisation, in the urban context of the waste picker community can be clearly analysed via the following media: resistance; vulnerability; breakdown of kinship and ethnic familial bonding under the influence of migration; peripheral existence; alternative social life; and patterns of consumption. Each of these areas I have closely studied in my work with the waste pickers, and I will examine each of them in turn, but first, a few more (very relevant) words about repression.

The nature of resistance

My ethnography (2011–13) suggests that any new agenda of any state should include all emerging sources of citizenship and the issue of their repression. Multiple causes are deemed responsible for the insurgence of marginalised people, which include: huge migration to the important cities of the world, unemployment, de-industrialisation, sexual revolution and democratisation (Holston 2008, 2009). The re-territorialisation of this huge new marginalised community within the city – with its own histories, cultures and demands disrupting the assumed categories of existing urban life – has resulted in new spaces of insurgent citizenship – the waste pickers – that execute a special kind of diverse and everyday resistance. The nature of their resistance is pervasive, passive and virtually unbeatable because it does not openly challenge the basic structure of domination, or contest the hierarchy, and it never escalates into any major open conflict with the opposition. Acts of resistance serve more to confer immediate advantages such as money or material gain, and deny long-term resource appropriation. Most often, the waste pickers practise passive non-compliance, subtle sabotage, evasion and deception in their activities – there is no inventiveness required. They use inbuilt and calculated prudence and secrecy, masked by the deference and conformity that is their regular public posture. It has to be so: open defiance is foolish for any community weaker than its weaker opposition and insubordination in almost any context would provoke a rapid and ferocious response.

Depending on the circumstances the waste pickers change their level of resistance, 'oscillating from rare organised acts to general silent and anonymous acts' (Scott 1985: 300). Whether it is against police harassment, a state oblivious to their welfare system, mainstream society's denial of their rights, or biased price negotiations and resource sharing with the retailers, resistance is usually individualistic and anonymous. It generally lacks organisation and co-ordination and is not linked with outside political and ideological movements; there are no 'elements of riots, demonstration, arson and open violence' (Scott 1985). Part of the reason for this is the sprawling geographical nature of the waste picker community. Scattered across the different fringe areas of the city and formed from a diverse collection of lower classes from various economically poor regions, there is often a lack of discipline and leadership among the people. Even if the whole community is involved in resistance, it rarely takes the shape of a conventional social movement.

Furthermore, my ethnographic evidence suggests such avoidance of confrontation by the waste pickers is a self-conscious strategy: resistance with no formal organisation, no formal leaders, no manifestos, no dues, no name and no banner may well work in the people's favour. By virtue of their institutional invisibility and the small scale of their activities, they are not usually noticed at all and rarely accorded any social significance (Scott 2009). And, nowadays, more conscious of their rights and of state schemes, concealing their contempt is essential for their survival. It is then, deliberate, that the waste picking community hides its rage in front of both the waste retailers and the outside world, even when they are underpaid. For example, the waste pickers will join feasts given by the retailers and NGOs even when they are very angry about their exclusion from their right-based schemes. The downside of this 'inaction' is the subsequent tendency to vent their anger in their family life, a subject discussed in detail below.

There is a second explanation for why, even in the face of continuous discrimination and prejudice from the state and mainstream society, the waste picker community never breaks out into a major riot. Put simply, marginalised people accept discrimination as their destiny. Their social defamation, indignity and cultural degradation influence them to take negative recourses into demoralisation and dysfunctionality. Instead of revolt, they avenge their anger by dissociating themselves from their neighbours, restricting their networks (even with NGOs) and they retreat from joint activities and building any movements. 'This social withdrawal and symbolic misidentification, in turn, undermine their local cohesion, hamper collective mobilisation and help to generate the very atomism that the dominant discourse on zones of urban dispossession claims is one of their inherent features' (Wacquant 2010b). Marginalised people are apparently mute about their intention, but research, my own included, rightly questions it. The rich retailers and mainstream society/elites repackage the huge economic disparity between them and the marginalised people as status, prestige and social control by using acts of generosity and charity. These acts are gentle, hidden forms of exploitation and are well sustained by the opposition, who must design their social authority link after link by means of strategic gifts, charity, loans, sociability, feasts and other concrete and symbolic services. When the opposition fail in this department, the marginalised people accuse them of meanness.

My ethnography (2011–13) observes that the opposition's fear about marginal people in terms of local power relations is not baseless, but the difference is, the waste retailers, mainstream/elites and the state are free to talk or take action whenever and however they want, but the marginalised waste pickers are largely forced to listen to them. The state, the retailers and the mainstream society/elites in contrast know less about the waste pickers' hidden and masked script. As a result, they suspect them more easily of things such as 'anonymous thefts, slander, ingratitude, and dissimulating' (Scott 2009). Specifically, in the waste picking community, retailers sometimes cut costs by hiring lorries and heavy vehicles in place of marginal people who are the main suppliers of wastes. They also raise the waste pickers' shelter rents, dismiss the waste pickers and cut back on ceremonial and charitable obligations within the community. This leads to an ideological vacuum and frustration for the marginalised community. The rich retailers and owners of recycling units have invented these creative methods to bend the facts of the case to suit their own causes. This violates the general rules of negotiation between all marginalised people and their employers. The moral context of the set of expectations (cast in the idioms of patronage, assistance, consideration and helpfulness) breaks down. Whenever the rich employers/retailers fail in giving assistance, advance wages, gifts, kindness, sympathy and in inviting to feasts, the retailers are treated with disrespect, disloyalty and social unrecognition by the marginalised people (Scott 1985). The potential for (mutual) exploitation is great, and there is no linguistic shortage when it comes to expressing the notion. I agree with Scott (1985), who quotes a phrase used in daily conversation: 'to eat – to eat our bones – to eat their sweat'. The easiest interpretation is that: 'he wants to eat us'. It is a powerful, suggestive metaphor, used not only by the waste pickers to describe what is done to them by the powerful retailers but is also used by the rich retailers to describe the demands for loans and charity pressed on them by the community.

Marginalised people, the waste pickers included, often express their feelings about the opposition through the concepts of stinginess and arrogance about the opposition. The waste pickers may not use the expression of eating but will say that the opposition is stingy, greedy and proud/arrogant. An individual waste picker whose request for a loan or charity from a retailer has been refused may not say directly or publicly that his employer is oppressing him, but will not fail to complain that the retailer is tight-fisted and without shame. These terms and metaphors are used by the waste pickers for accusing the retailers but they constitute the core of folk concepts of exploitation (Scott 2009). This usage of metaphors in collection constitutes a layer of ideological battle between the opposition and marginal. Thus the waste pickers can build up very passive ideological resistance against their opposition. On the other hand the opposition can push them to the extreme edge where they feel vulnerable and sometimes lose the tools needed to build up their tacit/passive resistance. As such, it is possible to distinguish between the strategies and key characteristics of the waste pickers and the opposition. Generosity, stinginess, arrogance, humility and wealth symbolise the opposition. Humility, help, assistance and poverty symbolise the people of the marginalised community.

Vulnerability of the marginalised community

Although the waste pickers can create new rules and tacit resistance to evade state control quite successfully, their vulnerability cannot be denied. They are under a constant physical threat of deportation or being forced to leave the city.

The state exploits the illegal status of these marginal non-citizens, who, in consequence, are paid very little. The waste pickers work for the urban population, clearing garbage from public spaces, which the state cannot do efficiently, but in return they are not offered membership of the mainstream society. In retaliation, they discover new and diverse forms of illegality and non-formalities. This unstable juxtaposition of legal opposition and illegal marginalised people weaving a network of multiplicity as regards the law shakes the state justice system and its framework of uniform law. Thus a body of overlapping, heterogeneous, non-uniform and private membership emerges in support of the non-citizens (Appadurai and Holston 1999).

The state and the mainstream/elite society also get support from other authorities (like police and jurisdiction) through 'privatisation of security and extra-legalisation of justice', which harshly and brutally controls the marginal (Appadurai 1996b). 'Justice' via private security and enforcers alongside the state's extra-legal police strength is used to try to take full control of these illegal waste pickers, who are thus exploited in the name of protection. This kind of violence has a deep effect on constitutional justice and the entire process of democracy with its highly esteemed concept of citizenship (Appadurai 2002; Holston 2009). The state is overwhelmed by the concept that it is all powerful, beyond any question. It can ignore, exclude or sometimes include powerless/dominated people within its framework but the state ignores the fact that it, too, can be ignored by the powerless waste pickers and they can survive independently of the state in terms of the economic, socio-cultural and religious aspects of their lives. (Bourdieu 1989) The marginalised waste pickers, on the other hand, feel completely ignored, excluded and deprived of their basic rights by the state; it is at this stage that they create their alternative position. They steal garbage; they earn money without paying taxes; they hook electricity illegally; they occupy state land (the so-called no-man's land). The state is either egalitarian or, in order to withhold a share of rights and resources from them, the state excludes the community from any mainstream activities. This suggests both that the state is uninterested in making marginalised people part of this public consumption/civil services and that the state is not neutral in its distribution and redistribution of basic amenities, which fall under the category of public consumption. The whole system for distribution and redistribution of citizens' tax money for education, health, shelter, sanitation, food rationing and banking is bureaucratic and biased against marginal people.

The making of urban peripheries

The waste pickers are typical of marginal people who almost never use violence to claim their spaces; they always occupy the public spaces of modern cities that have been abandoned. They can never touch 'the residential enclaves, the division of corporate luxury zones'. At most, they appropriate spaces that are 'forbidden sectors of illegally constructed shanties, with its endless neighbourhoods of unemployed youth' (Appadurai and Holston 1996). Cities like Calcutta, therefore, experience the most significant crisis of state membership and the civic authorities understand that state and civil society must rethink the concept of citizenship. It has been claimed that the extraordinary urbanisation of the twentieth century has produced urban peripheries of devastating poverty and proportionate inequality in cities worldwide (Holston 2009). All people, like the waste pickers, who live in these urban peripheries struggle to obtain basic resources for daily life and shelter. These struggles, in turn, give rise to insurgent citizenship which tries to acquire rights within cities, which are very weak and full of dichotomies. Holston (2009: 245) marks this phenomenon as 'new kinds of citizen power and social justice'. The 'insurgent urban citizenships' contain both inequality and new forms of destabilisation and violence. The waste pickers build up fragile shelters in urban fringes, which are illegal and irregular in nature. In these situations they confront extreme inequality and segregation from urban institutions in terms of religion, culture, health care, shelter and education. It is certainly my experience that not all peripheries/fringe areas produce insurgence, but they definitely produce some form of collision and conflict (Holston 2009). In the long run, the waste pickers – these 'marginalised citizens and non-citizens' – contest their volatile conditions and the regular exclusions they face. Thus they disrupt the established norms of 'urban democratic citizenship'. This disruption is clearly the projection of their peripheries/marginal positions.

The mainstream/elite civic society strategically segregates public life so that 'the urban poor in the peripheries' are pushed to a bare life of servility (Scott 2009: 246). 'The structures of inequality incite these hinterland residents to demand a life worthy of citizens' (Holston 2009: 246). In my ethnography I frequently debate how far these 'non-citizens' of waste pickers can articulate their demands with force and 'originality'. Rather their struggle forms in order to cope with their daily, domestic life in the remote urban peripheries. In spite of daily struggles for housing, sanitation and security they do not even receive the dignity of 'bare citizens'. Further, they are sequestered in areas away from the elite centre, creating a different order of citizenship and exclusion. These uprooted and dispossessed marginalised people in the context of twentieth and twenty-first century urbanisation have helped to develop urban peripheries as their own place in the city by their signature irregular, illegal types of shelter and ways of life. They appropriate this soil of the city and demand the right to inhabit it. They also pronounce their 'right to reside with dignity, security and mobility'.

I contest the point that these marginal/non-citizens even have an appropriate awareness about their rights, dignity, security and mobility (Ethnography 2011–13). I agree that these marginalised people with 'horrific urban conditions' (Holston 2009: 249), are left with very little room for dignity and vitality. The waste pickers are autonomous in nature. They have been denied political rights, excluded from property ownership, estranged from law, incorporated into nonformal labour market as servile workers and forced into segregated and illegal conditions of residence in a remote no-man's land that is devoid of any infrastructure. The situation is paradoxical in the sense that marginalised communities can keep their freedom, as they are completely cut off from the centre/state and are situated in the interior-remoteness, but for this freedom they must exchange their dignity and basic state welfare schemes.

If we take up Bourdieu's (1989: 56) deduced theory which says that if the state is X which successfully claims a monopoly of the legitimate use of physical and symbolic power over a definite territory and majority of the population, then the waste pickers are subverting the whole scheme (Ethnography 2011–13). Their exclusion and non-participation breaks the notion of interdependency between citizens and the state (Bourdieu 1989). The extreme non-participation and exclusion of marginalised people in state/NGO programmes can be explained as subversion and as the breaking down of the power structure through which the state and the elite/mainstream society operates (Ethnography 2011–13). It follows from this that the construction of the state supports the construction of a field of power. It also defines the space of play within which the holders of capital struggle in particular for power over the different dimensions of the process (state). The different dimensions of this process (state) – armed forces, taxation, law, etc. – are interdependent (Bourdieu 1989a), but I will show later on that the waste picker community is outside this interdependency.

Kinship and social relations

The lack of external support is liable to have a knock-on effect within a community; when abandoned by infrastructures and civic amenities, kinship and familial bonding frequently break down in the neighbourhoods of marginalised people; many urban communities become relatively unstable in their networks of kinship, friendship, work and leisure, as well as in terms of birth, residence and other filial forms (Appadurai 1996a). Such is measurably evident in the waste picker community. After their migration from villages to city (which, in itself, imposes a very different kind of life on them) classical kinship becomes volatile. New commodity patterns are negotiated, debts and obligations resettled, and rumours and fantasies about the new setting manoeuvred into existing systems of knowledge and practice. This becomes a huge strain on marriages in general and on women in particular – marriage being the meeting points of historical patterns of socialisation. The work of cultural reproduction is profoundly complicated, especially for the young generation as they try hard to represent their family as 'normal' to their neighbourhood and peer group in their new locale. At the same time, the family environment can be problematic due to trauma created by the dispossession from their roots and origins and disconnection from their village family pool. Appadurai (1996b) calls this the fractured spatial arrangements.

The women within the waste picker community take almost total responsibility for their families, and in so doing have to negotiate increasingly harsh working conditions both at home and in non-domestic workplaces. In short, my ethnography (2011–13) shows that this de-territorialised community may enjoy some of the fruits of new kinds of earning but it will equally gain a new kind of disjointed kinship and suffer from unfulfilled desires and fantasies. Such desires and fantasies are the products of gambling, addiction and strong mediation (television and cheap video films). I would agree with Appadurai, who is critical about apparent happiness and mirage of choices in the lives of urban marginalised people. He confirms my findings: ironically, the waste pickers' lives have become more miserable and hopeless. They are partially governed by the conventions of the Hindi films and mainstream media culture, through which they try to feel the excitement of life; they have their own image, ideas and dreams. Although brutality, dehumanisation and inequality have taken every chance to exploit the waste pickers' lives, still they can be manipulated by a compromise between what they can imagine film-like, and what their real life permits. The reality of life for these urban marginal people and their agonised drama of leisure are inadequate to cover their anxieties and self-abasement (Appadurai 1996a).

Newly-settled families, especially the children of the waste pickers, face daily risk in perpetuating their own culture and so demonstrate apparent eagerness to leave behind their own traditions and come under the strong grip of mainstream culture. This is referred to as the 'mechanical art' and 'disjuncture' by Holston (2008). In the long run, the shape of their culture becomes 'less bounded, tacit and more fluid' (Appadurai 2006a). The waste pickers lack the spirit and structure of kinship and become disarrayed, therefore lacking the courage to do violence in mainstream public spaces – but the inclination does not fade. Their violence simply becomes limited and 'embedded in the fabric of local networks of exchange and status' (Wacquant 2008: 213). The – primarily male – waste pickers apply violence within their families until it becomes an intensive social practice. The sociability of the family unit often turns violent and physical force is asserted on women by men (Wacquant 2008). The type of violence in the fabric of the community's family lives is categorised as a source of nagging annoyance rather than 'ubiquitous danger' (Wacquant 2008: 213). This perception is a reflection of their constant fear engendered by the dominance of their informal economy and the breakdown of public welfare, alongside their fractured private, local and social relationships. That said, on the rare occasions the waste pickers do show their anger against state and mainstream biases, this anger acts as a catalyst to criminalise them. They lose their human rights and implicitly help the police to carry out violence upon them. For example, the waste picking people regularly handle garbage late at night that is the property of the government: this is illegal and invites police violence against them. The illegal actions and occupation of the waste pickers transform the normative order of urban mainstream/elite social life into a rawness, outrage and exaggeration, which in summation can be called incivility on the part of the marginal people. This incivility has been described in research as a 'public idiom of resistance and insistence' (Holston 2009: 263).

Uprooted from their original shelter, family pool, kinship and myths, the waste pickers do not belong to any territory and are mobile in nature. They come from different social networks, mainly from rural areas, and form a community in an urban setting that gives rise to new kinds of politics, a very unique kind of collective expression (of stoicism, passiveness and disconnectedness) and a new need for social discipline (Wacquant 2008: Urban Outcasts). Since they consider themselves guest workers in the city, so they are barely noticeable in any discourse of proper social life. Also, they do not participate in any kinship practices except some religious and ritualistic functions and ceremonies in the neighbourhood (Appadurai 2006a). The question, then, arises as to how they manage their lives in lieu of participating in social and kinship practices? The fundamental answer lies in the fact that they create an alternative social life: for female waste pickers this centres around the family unit, but the men congregate together and this is where alcohol, gambling and drugs frequently become leisure activities and segue into addiction and anti-social behaviour within their own community. This is something I have seen first-hand on a number of occasions.

The alternative social life of the marginalised people

Certainly some of the root causes of the waste pickers' problems are in their displacement, political and other institutional and organisational abandonment and lack of kinship. But at the same time these root causes act as a catalyst in their life, creating dreams of wealth, respectability and autonomy. These retain the tension between global and local (their city life in reality) that creates their cultural reproduction at present (Appadurai 1996a). Parents and children in the waste picker community opt for non-formal schools – if they attend at all; a huge issue for the NGO-provision – which comprise overcrowded facilities staffed by under-trained and under-paid teachers, with outdated and grossly insufficient supplies (Wacquant 2008). I have seen how the children have no separate classrooms; all age groups sit in the same room and their non-formal classrooms lack infrastructures like chairs, drinking water, toilet facilities and libraries. Wacquant (2008) says that marginalised children do not have laboratories for scientific experiments or working photocopying machines, and indeed, the waste picking children do not consider these materials in their wildest dreams (Ethnography 2011–13). How do the children and parents battle against such an absence of infrastructure? In reality they learn to adjust to such conditions. The neighbourhoods cope without public (state-sponsored) or private formal schools and without cinemas, museums or public libraries. I learned that the waste pickers are even sometimes unaware of these kinds of infrastructural facilities because NGOs in their neighbourhood run their projects with 'miserly budgets' and cannot provide any such attractions for the community. It has been observed that public (state) policies aim to 'devalorize' public welfare for marginalised people so that they return to their native villages (Wacquant 2008: 222).

While the state would like marginalised people to discover their own 'exit points' (Wacquant 2008: 222), my ethnography (2011–13) demonstrates that the community people have no such doors (real or metaphorical) by which to leave the 'sinking ship' (Wacquant 2008:222) of their squatter settlement. Calcutta, like all big cities, may have developed many 'banks, stylish hotels, department stores, night clubs, cinemas, posh lounges and beauty parlours' (Wacquant 2008: 223) but the waste picker settlements have minimal shops supplying illegal country liquor, makeshift clubs, cheap clothing shops and some family-owned eateries. This reveals the biased role of the state and 'public policies in fashioning the institutions and public spaces' (Wacquant 2008: 223) which prevent the community from accessing the social safety nets woven by the state authority. They are not even allowed to contribute significantly to social networking or the political system. This is why the waste pickers organise their own social life and create a new space for its participation (non-formal occupations, education, health care, markets, a makeshift system of sanitation and rights for themselves).

Such new civic participation generates three types of experiences among the peripheral groups (Holston 2009). The first is a new means of participation in an alternative public sphere where the waste pickers may attempt to pronounce their needs for a new agenda of citizenship. Second, they are able to gain a broader understanding of their dignity and rights. The third experience they gather is an unconventional interpretation of the relationship between themselves and the state. 'The very conditions of remoteness in the peripheries enabled an off-work and out of sight freedom to invent new modes of association' for these marginal people (Holston 2009).

In-civic (not demanding basic services from the state) expressions of insurgent citizenship can be seen as forms of protest and disruption in response to the exclusion that they frequently face (Holston 2009). The waste pickers feel that elite/mainstream society looks at them not as new additions, but as trespassers inside their public and domestic spaces. In retaliation, from the peripheries, they impose their own distance from the elite/mainstream society, instigated by their fear, suspicion and outrage. The community withdraws from the mainstream society/elites in their everyday personal contact, and this becomes their signature living condition. Further, they also develop new social and physical barriers.

As I have already touched upon, bureaucratic bias creates apathy and frustration among some marginalised people; in the waste picker community, the men are particularly prone to these emotions (or certainly most likely to act upon them) and this apathy and frustration can take the shape of periodic outbursts of violence (Wacquant 2008). Interestingly, though, in my ethnography (2011–13), the collapse of public institutions is actually the leading cause of systematic physical and social insecurity. This collapse has led to the extensive decomposition of the organisational fabric of the marginalised neighbourhoods, following the ebb of the civil rights movements. This decomposition, in turn, diminishes opportunities, shrinking the set of viable life strategies and instead stimulating individual strategies of internal predation that further accelerate 'the decline' (Wacquant 2008: 224) of the squatter settlement of the waste pickers (Ethnography 2011–13).

Consumption and economic marginalisation

The acts of consumption that surround the waste pickers' routine often proves less mechanical than that of their opposition. The exchange of gifts and transactions among families in marriages and during festivals is regulated by an extremely complex set of strategic interactions, which are unpredictable. The basic package of rites dealing with birth, initiation, marriage and death is usually regarded as a cultural regularity with a remarkable degree of universality of owing and gift exchanges. But what marks the waste picker community as different is the almost total lack of social visibility, very low-key monetary-material transactions, and the 'very poor level' of consumption and exchanges in these events. Their consumption levels, during any festival and the main natural rites and rituals, are quite low. In these small, low-tech societies the quantitative explosion associated with the world of commodity has not yet appeared. Yet, their particular conjunctures of commodity flow and trade can create unprecedented and unusual changes in value structures (Appadurai 2002). The marginalised waste pickers do not have a concept of vacation and in the urban setting they see themselves as constrained and time-restricted individuals. It is for this reason the waste pickers value their production and leisure time only in terms of money, and they go through their unique kind of fantasy (the television programmes, cheap video shows, drugs and gambling and sometimes pure alternative games and sports as enjoyed by both children and adults), which make them completely devoid of any education and project training. The adults have relayed to me how they feel irritated at the concept of leisure time, creative activities or any project-oriented activities as suggested by the NGO.

Modern mainstream urban people enhance their buying power in the face of huge salary differences by borrowing money in the form of loans from different financial institutions and through the plastic credit system (Appadurai 1996a). It is easy to be highly critical about the whole system because citizens end up facing huge, brutal interest rates, which are almost catalytic in collapsing their 'recent savings and creating loan catastrophes' (Appadurai 2006a) and this attractive and apparently flexible artificial purchasing power, ultimately profits banks and business houses while putting immense pressure on urban household incomes to repay these loans. If there is a curious 'upside' to this, it is that the waste picker community cannot be infected; if it does not enjoy access to an institutional banking system, neither can it face the problematic and difficult situations endemic to the plastic card system. The waste pickers' natural austerity combined with their lower consumption power means they do not fall under the radar of the ruthless banking and corporate sphere, and so avoid the peculiar tension arising out of the uncertainty about procuring money for purchasing commodities. As such, they miss out on the tension of consumer debt management, the gigantic struggle and the rival misunderstanding between urban consumers and money lending institutions (credit cards and bank loans). True, local money-lenders may harass them for repayments, but such systems ultimately have a human face and they are removed from the ugly visage of state and corporate financial harassment.

On the downside, the negative effects of this phenomenon are that the waste pickers cannot access even the simplest banking procedure or plan any institutional financial scheme. Consequently, they do not save any money for their future. Instead, they (especially the males of the community) spend everything on gambling, betting, alcohol, unhealthy food habits, cheap dresses, drugs and other pleasures such as hiring videos jointly to watch cheap films, songs and dance sequences and visiting sex workers. In turn, they have less money for their children's education, and they can never think about more structured sanitation, hygienic food habits, health and medical care or shelter conditions. Women pickers often try to join some projects for the benefit of their children, but they are almost always unsuccessful as their male counterparts fail to support them. The irony is that the waste picking community hangs in limbo between modernity (in a very loose and hodgepodge sense, as the members live in urban fringes and have unfulfilled consumerist desires built upon television advertisements) but are equally non-consumers in banking, credit and loan terms. While safe from the harassment of the state and corporate banks, they are deprived of state education, sanitation, health care and housing projects. This lack of access to civic infrastructures puts them in an angry mindset and their anger leads them to their unique style of participation.

Struggles for urban infrastructures ignite new kinds of organisations and strategic thinking among these squatters and it is possible that urban marginal people form friendship with NGOs, the middle classes and international groups in the hope of creating a new kind of 'Indian democracy' (Appadurai 2002). In the case of my research and the experience of the waste picker community (Ethnography 2011–13), this occurs from the opposite direction. The NGOs, the mainstream society/elites, and the international groups try to form allegiances with the marginalised people on the peripheries to further the interests of ongoing international projects, as well as those of the marginalised people. This is demonstrated by the way that the NGOs are eagerly trying to bring the marginalised people into the different projects and networks, including the Waste Pickers' Association. Mainstream society/elites often try to give them their own recyclable waste in order to overcome their guilt about preventing marginal people from sharing the main material and cultural resources. On the other hand, the marginalised community keeps itself outside the state and mainstream public spaces and benefits. The book further emphasises that segregation pushes these people hard to demand inclusion in the legal city, its property, infrastructure and services. These mobilisations create a great deal of awareness among marginal people. Surprisingly enough (quite contrary to my field report findings) the subjects of Holston's study demand urbanisation, forcing the state to provide infrastructure and access to health services, schools, public lighting, bus services and childcare. In my own ethnography (2011–13) the waste pickers never demanded such services from the state, although they sometimes asked for them from the NGO.

In summary, my ethnography with the waste pickers of Calcutta, framed within existing literature and anthropological theories, shows how and why marginalised people tend to live in areas where social and economic problems gather and grow. The waste pickers are, in fact, typical. They are called various names, such as 'outcasts' (Wacquant 2008:1), non-elites, non-citizens, insurgent citizens, marginal, marginalised, anti-socials, moral outsiders, parasites, depressed, pariahs and submerged (Amborn 1990; Appadurai 1996a, 1996b, 2006a; Appadurai and Holston 1999; Arnold 1993, 1995a, 1995b; Holston 2008, 2009; Pankhurst 2003) by the elites/mainstream society and the state. Further the book adds that marginalised people are described as the weak, the religiously deviant, the uprooted and the illegitimate (Appadurai 2002, 2006a). The waste picking community has been symbolically evaluated as the uncivilised and without history (Appadurai 2002, 2006a). The areas where they live acquire bad reputations and huge 'negative attention' (Wacquant 2008: 1) from the state, mainstream/elite societies and politicians (who, together, form the 'opposition' in my ethnography). The places in which marginalised people live are identified, to the opposition, as the 'lawless zones, problem estates, the no-go areas or the wild districts of the cities' (Wacquant 2008: 1). The marginalised areas are places of 'deprivation' and 'dereliction' and to a greater or lesser extent anthropologists find that these places with bad reputations are 'hotbeds of violence, vice and social dissolution' (Wacquant 2008: 1).

In closing this chapter, my extensive use of quotes is deliberate and somewhat superfluous. Fundamentally, the terminology used is immaterial: whatever phrases are employed, whatever reasons given, however we define the key concepts, it is clear that communities like the waste pickers of Calcutta are entirely excluded from the mainstream of society. Beyond any economic marginalisation that they may be faced with, the communities are also unambiguously ideologically marginalised, particularly in terms of culture and religion.

Note

1 In subsequent chapters, they will provide context for the ethnographic research, enabling an understanding of the daily experiences of material dilapidation, physical seclusion, ideological marginalisation, socio-economic marginality translated into the decay of the self, the breakdown of interpersonal and neighbourhood ties through the mediation of the biased state, and mainstream/elite policies attached to these defamed peripheral regions (Wacquant 2010a).

3 Ideological marginalisation versus economic marginalisation

For the waste pickers of Calcutta, ideological and economic marginalisation are different in nature. Existing anthropological theories and ethnographic narratives have focused on both types of marginalisation (Arnold 1993, 1995a, 1995b; Kelly 1991; Pankhurst 1999, 2003) and the dominant view is of the primary source being economic, which leads to ideological marginalisation through the active or passive processes that occur between the state/elite/mainstream society and the marginalised community. It is my contention that for the waste pickers, ideological marginalisation is the outcome of an attempted escape route from economic marginalisation, demonstrated in this book, through an analysis of the dialectics between the invisibility of the waste pickers inside their tightly-closed, opaque, illegal, non-formal world, and the visibility of the apparently transparent state/elite/mainstream society. As such, ideological marginalisation, embodied in silent defiance and subtle negotiation by a marginalised people, gives a premise distinctly separate from economic marginalisation.

Existing theories illustrate how marginal people create uncertainties and tension in national identity and citizenship, establishing their own voices and choices in different dimensions of marginalisation. They further demonstrate how the state/elite/mainstream justify and negotiate marginalisation with marginalised groups. (Appadurai 1986, 1988, 1996a, 1996b, 2002, 2006a, 2006b; Appadurai and Holston 1996; Bourdieu and Wacquant 1992; Scott 1985, 1990, 2009). In analysing the story of the waste picking community, I can reveal how, in spite of countering economic marginalisation efficiently, this community is forced to succumb to ideological marginalisation as schemed by the state/elite/mainstream society. In addition, since ideological marginalisation takes the lead role over economic, the waste pickers are unable to progress in their business of waste picking. Situated in the two squatter settlements of Topsia and Park Circus, I have already described how this predominantly Muslim community is engaged in the specialised occupation of non-formal waste picking. Specifically, it begins with rubbish collection, after which the recyclable waste is segregated from the general and sold to waste retailers, who, in turn, sell it to recycling units. From there, it is converted to recycled products. As such, the work of the waste picking community forms part of the (informal) solid waste management system of the region. The economics involved are considered to be underground, or 'black money'.

In examining the history of recycling, it is clear that waste picking and segregation started as an art, within which waste pickers have the eyes of jewellers. It is the outsider who views waste as waste rather than the valuable scraps seen by the waste pickers. When a modern shopkeeper uncaringly discards 'rubbish' onto the street, these waste pickers retrieve it as recyclable metal – items containing copper, iron and aluminium are worth a lot of money. One management representative told me, 'We throw away our batteries but they (the waste pickers) can extract the costly metals even from tiny materials. They go for scraps of bigger portions of metals as well.'

The history of waste picking goes back 80–90 years, but migration of those involved in such work has increased as the quantities of recyclable waste have become greater with modern life. Those having travelled independently to Calcutta, in search of jobs, find themselves forced, by lack of other options, into the waste picking profession. Frequently, though, workers are solicited by agents who visit the rural villages deliberately. They target parents who have five or six unwanted children and promise them that they will bring the children to the city of Calcutta and engage them in a nice, dignified profession. In reality, they take the children to waste picking communities, and other factories, as child labour. The children then learn the profession of waste segregation very efficiently. Later, their parents join them. According to one functionary of an NGO, life for these migrant children becomes even more depressing. In village life there is less food and its nutritional quality is lower, but the environment is devoid of criminal activities and addiction, and as such is a much healthier and safer environment for children to grow up in compared to Calcutta. It is worth remembering, too, that while migrants move from their rural homes to the urban life primarily for the social and economic freedom built upon rubbish segregation (such freedoms that could not be achieved if they remained in their rural setting of unemployment and severe hunger), there are other determining factors. The destruction of homes through natural disasters like floods or cyclones; family conflicts, including disputes over property (for example being driven out of the house by in-laws after becoming a widow); the selling of their land and other properties to pay debts (e.g. medical treatment, or providing dowries for their daughters' marriages) that leave them penniless. These rural migrants, especially, experience a new kind of hope and disillusionment, imagination and frustration, fear and despair. Either they create, improvise or are dominated in terms of their own new imagination, or they are left standing in a new environment without any history, myth or imagination as insurgent citizens excluded from urban planning, government and the social fabric.

Over the last 40–60 years, the waste pickers settling in Park Circus originate from West Bengal, the majority (90 per cent) from South 24 Parganas and others from Canning, Jibantala, Basanti, Gosaba, Lakhikantapur, Charan, Jhar Khali, Kalidanga and Sundarban. Those established in Topsia (in Mir Meher Ali Lane) arrive from Uttar Pradesh, Bihar and Bangladesh. My ethnography (2010–13) shows that almost all of the older generation of this specific group have been here for the last 56 years; their children and grandchildren were born and brought up in the city settlements. All are Bengali-speaking Muslims, but they have Hindi-speaking neighbours. From these neighbours and Bollywood films they pick up Hindi and try to speak in that language, and some of them are able to speak Urdu as well. The waste pickers have moved, en masse, from an agricultural to an urban set up; from a non-waged position to a non-formal structure of wage-earning in the (also non-formal) recycling chain. On average, a family with three children can earn 250–300 rupees (€4–5) per day in this informal market where they create their own capital, but while these families no longer have monetary problems, their whole socio-cultural environment is transformed and set in an unethical, criminal setting. The women still invest in family matters and the welfare of their children. However, the men, reacting to the high price of escape from marginalisation, tend to invest in gambling and drug addiction. Such behaviours, fuelled by their inbuilt mistrust of mainstream society, lead the male waste pickers to develop non-conformist attitudes, thus demonstrating their own power to challenge the state. As such, the main crisis is no longer economic in nature; it becomes moral. Young boys venture deep into addiction, and as soon as they reach adolescence, they become involved with the criminals who ultimately control their lives.

My ethnographic evidence concerning the people of Topsia and Park Circus backs up all the hypothetical presentations of marginalised communities as outlined in Chapter 2. The waste pickers' history of exclusion and their limited communication skills curtail contact with mainstream society. Further, their lack of integration with the outside economy encourages the illegal establishment of an 'inside' underground version. The community is also without access to civic institutions – they have a very small mosque (apparently not recognisable as such) and a club (a makeshift room containing mats and chairs). Such damaged lives and fragmentation ultimately escalates the recognised cycle of mental and physical violence within families and the immediate neighbourhood. Thus, this business of rubbish segregation, although economically viable on a small scale, makes the waste pickers eternally 'impure' on so many levels. In fact, my findings demonstrate that the ideological marginalisation of this community has gone so far as to be virtually irreparable. The waste pickers feel like non-citizens, undeserving of the attention and care of Calcutta Corporation and other local authorities. They will not leave their shelters in the no-man's land unless they are evicted; they will tolerate their utter material discomfort (such as poor quality drinking water and the absence of sanitation and shelter). They are even reluctant to invest any money in education or to send their children to school. State welfare has been replaced by aggression from the police, the legal system, the general public and commercial spaces; banks, for example. Whenever this community cannot resolve its own problems – minor conflicts or bigger issues involving violence or crime – the mainstream society/elite blames it for its own predicaments. Not only is this a clear indication of why the waste pickers try so hard to be invisible and make no attempt to come into mainstream focus, it has greater ramifications. For instance, when the chief functionary of an NGO states that the government record shows the number of waste pickers has decreased, the truth is that, on the contrary, the whole waste picking business is simply continuing and increasing, unrecorded. NGO staff member Kashmira Khatoon specifically raises the question of the exact number of waste pickers in the city of Calcutta, suggesting that there should be a thorough census and research conducted jointly by the NGOs and the state. Her intention is to evidence a clear idea of how many waste pickers the state must accommodate in their welfare schemes. However, it is an added complication that the waste pickers themselves try to avoid these welfare schemes in order to escape from the disciplinary rules of the state and the stern gaze of the elite/mainstream society.

The waste picker's settlement

Calcutta is a big city with a huge population; one can travel for hours without the slightest hint that there are two fringe squatter settlements within reach, one beside a polluted canal (Narkeldanga and Topsia) and the other along the Park Circus railway tracks. The waste pickers have no privacy, no individual addresses. Their poverty has been assigned a separate, communal territory – removed from the sight of the happier classes – where they struggle as best they can. At best, makeshift dwellings, clothing and food are the remuneration given to the waste picker by an unknown and non-formal society. The most inadequate shelters are in the worst quarters of the city and almost always irregularly built. The streets are generally crooked and narrow, unpaved, rough and dirty, filled with vegetable and animal refuse, without sewers or gutters, but supplied with foul, stagnant pools. Ventilation is impeded by the confused method of building, and since many human beings live crowded into this small space, the prevailing atmosphere is suffocating. The streets serve as drying grounds in fine weather; lines are stretched across from shelter to shelter, and hung with wet clothing.

A vegetable market is held in the street; baskets full of vegetables and fruits – all bad and hardly fit for consumption – obstruct the sidewalk still further, and from these and the fish-dealers' stalls arises a horrible smell. The shelters are filthy, within and without, and their appearance is such that no human being would want to live in them. But all this is nothing in comparison with the dwellings in the narrow alleys between the 'main' streets inhabited by the poorest of the poor; the worst paid and most disorganised waste pickers with anti-socials and the victims of prostitution indiscriminately huddled together. Those who have not yet sunk in the whirlpool of moral ruin which surrounds them sink deeper daily, increasingly losing the power to resist the demoralising influence of want and filth. Entered by covered passages between the shelters, the filth and ruin of the alleyways surpass all description. Heaps of rubbish and ashes lie in all directions, and the foul liquids emptied out of the doors gather into cesspits. Scarcely a whole window-pane or door can be found and the bamboo walls are crumbling. Door posts and window frames are loose and broken, the doors themselves made of old boards nailed together, or wanting altogether. As there is nothing to steal, doors are not needed to prevent theft, but there are frequent incidents of rape and sexual harassment of younger girls in the community, and no doors means no security. Parents live in a permanent state of anxiety about the safety of their daughters; helpless to protect them from local and outside hoodlums, they generally prefer to marry them off at a very young age.

It is not uncommon for a waste picking couple with four or five waste picking children, and sometimes the grandfather and grandmother, to be found sleeping, eating and working in a room of 10–12 square feet. Each shelter has at least one bed (a kind of wooden plank) in a room, or as many as can fit. Into each bed four, five or six human beings are piled: sick and well, young and old, drunk and sober, men and women. Other family members lie down under the wooden plank. Such cramped conditions inevitably lead to arguments, blows, wounds or worse; thefts are arranged and things done which mainstream language refuses to record. Yet – it could be even worse. In spite of these conditions, sheltered families are fortunate in comparison with the utterly homeless. Those who cannot pay for such 'refuge' sleep wherever they find a place: in passages, in arcades and in corners. The police, club members and retailers have a vested interest in allowing them to remain undisturbed; the police receive regular bribes; the retailers receive a good quantity of waste for the recycling units; and the club members can make broader networks with NGOs and recycling units through the waste picking community.

Waste pickers are not allowed to set up home in existing slum areas, as they are considered to be pollutants and anyway, they would not choose to reside in the slums as they are very congested, and the slum dwellers do not allow them sufficient space to segregate their waste into general waste and recyclable waste. So, when looking for somewhere to build a shelter, the waste pickers always try to find abandoned, barren sites that are government property – no-man's lands, where no mainstream people will go for any purpose. The waste pickers can establish their temporary shelters on these lands for almost nothing, and if they can spend 3–4 years in the same place, it is their gain. In these squatter settlements, they are able to create their own makeshift spaces for their work – either inside their shelters or just outside. There is no such thing as 'no space'. In Field Area I, Nazma, one of the woman waste pickers from Topsia, related how some major fires had broken out on one side of the canal and forced the waste pickers to move to the other side and cram into their shelters somehow.

The community chooses to dwell near railway line/tracks as these offer good communication links. Very early in the morning the waste pickers can catch trains to travel long distances for refuge collection purposes, without buying tickets. Hamida, another female waste picker from Field Area I, also pointed out that the canal-side spaces give the community easy access to open-air toilets, which can only be cleaned with canal water. These toilets are unhygienic, but there is no other option. Even so, the squat, if sold, can fetch a high price – around €400–500. When the waste pickers are promoted to retailers, they sell off their squats and move to the slums (although this costs them considerably more). Some of them – albeit a small minority – after accumulating a certain amount of money, return to their villages to resume their agricultural life.

I have already drawn attention to the urban wasteland locations in which the waste pickers 'choose' their shelters: the fringe areas and the 'no-man's land'. Of course, there is little actual choice involved. The vibrant, bustling and commercial neighbourhood of Calcutta simply excludes and ignores this marginalised community, which, one of my informants (an NGO staff member) explained has been declared, by the government, a polluting factor in terms of both society and the environment. The waste picker community is omitted from 'the rise and birth of hundreds of commercial, social, and cultural establishments, from machine shops, beauty shops, hotels, posh houses, corporate hospitals and state health care, theatres and restaurants, temples, mosques and banks, clothing outlets and shopping malls' (Wacquant 2010b). The waste pickers' movements are severely restricted inside each of these areas, as well as within public hospitals, educational centres (apart from NGO-run non-formal schools), housing societies and parks in broad daylight. They cannot even use the proper roads and instead find their own roads and space to move their rubbish vans. Instead they stick to their private spaces in a situation not dissimilar to a prison or a ghetto (Wacquant 2010b). As a result, their meagre shelters, streets, work areas and informal market places look like 'the strip of burnt-out garbage space strewn with weeds, all sorts of garbage and broken glasses' (Wacquant 2010b).

The waste pickers' fundamental motive is to survive. They know they are living on illegal land; they know they can be evicted from their land and shelter any day. There is also the direct threat of eviction from the Railway Authority, which forces waste pickers to purchase small plots of land in the rural areas. Thus, the community can only think of its immediate reality; a reflection of its neglect and deprivation at the hands of the state and mainstream society. Information I received from the State Conservancy and Recycling Sector demonstrates how the Housing Development Corporation, Calcutta, provides cross subsidies for inexpensive shelters for deprived groups. The rich house owners are taxed more in order to provide the poor with some inexpensive huts. Yet a huge conflict is observed between the house owner (the state) and the tenants (the marginalised community). During the time of my ethnography (2011–13), the state evicted 300 waste picker families beside the Park Circus connector, giving them only €200 per squatter as compensation. This money percolated through the police, local clubs and mafia, leaving the waste pickers with nothing – as confirmed directly with me, by the police and club members. Therefore, 300 families just vanished from that area. Mr Alamgir, one of my field colleagues, related that the 300 families were constantly under the threat of eviction and had to go into hiding. The club secretary and members, and community leaders from their squatter areas, told the waste picker families they would not receive a single cent from the €200 and so should just disappear. Threatened with imminent eviction by the state and following a mysterious fire in the locality, the families were forced to leave the fringe areas. Only temporarily deterred, they returned on the other side of the canal and erected makeshift shelters there.

There is the floating perception that any waste picker who has the money may buy his or her own shelter. One advocate is the informant Chhad Banu, an upscale waste picker, who, along with her husband, possesses a van. Their shelter is quite shabby and broken down, very much in parity with other households in the vicinity beside the dark canal (into which sewage water runs). The wall comprises broken bamboo thatch, clothes and jute sacks; the roof is covered with plastic over a bamboo structure; they have illegally tapped electricity – although they continually face power cuts. When provided with a basic government-issue shelter, they rejected the proposal because the distance from the settlement to their work area was likely to jeopardise their profession and deprive them of earnings. Following their refusal, the head of the Government Conservancy section flatly advised the community people to go back to their villages; that is, to a world of greater poverty and potential starvation. Some NGO staff are critical of this, believing the state intentionally gave the waste pickers huts in remote areas, anticipating that they would not take any risks by moving away from the Dhapa or Calcutta roadside bins (the areas where most of the city waste is collected). The waste pickers refused to accept the offer.

Believing that a stigmatised community degrades not only itself but the entire neighbourhood, the state further justified its special measures 'of destabilising, further marginalising' the community, 'subjecting them to the dictates of the deregulated labour market, and rendering them invisible or driving them out of a coveted space' (Wacquant 2007a) by referring to the fringe area of the community as a 'lawless zone' or 'outlaw estate outside any common norm' (Wacquant 2007b). Thus, eviction was legitimated and, as the community lacked appropriate assets to participate in socio-political activities, dispossession from their no-man's land into a remote place should have been straightforward. In reality, though, the current community settlement is becoming one of those 'coveted areas', and a convenient city-based place for their work. The waste picker community's response is to exist quietly outside mainstream society in their current locations. Thus, we come full circle, for their shelters are precariously located along dangerous railway tracks, at high risk of accidents – including the early deaths of their children as they attempt to cross the railway lines in order to play or go to their non-formal schools – and beside the black, polluted canals of Narkeldanga; an exit point for city sewage.

The vicious circle of migration and marginalisation

It is, perhaps, inevitable that migration and marginalisation are something of a vicious circle. Migration causes social marginalisation, which creates more forced migration and increasing paranoia about the state among migrants, making them more marginalised. As a result, migrant people tend to build up 'self-propelling' ghettos with restricted movement and sometimes without any movement at all. The community produces or reproduces their own locality. They contract and celebrate marriages, birth and deaths; social and business contracts are made and honoured verbally without any legal documents; money is made and spent; goods are produced and exchanged within the group. This may, in the long run, give rise to a neighbourhood, which then probably does fall –

very loosely – within the purview of the state but despite this such community areas constitute the starkest examples of the conditions of uncertainty, poverty, displacement and despair. The lives and worlds of the waste pickers are produced in the darkest circumstances (Appadurai 1996a, 2006a). I would emphasise that such 'neighbourhoods' lack any name, and the population has the barest commitment to the production of the state. In order to avoid the unpleasant consequences that might be inflicted upon them by the state and elite society, these fringe-neighbourhoods move to more peaceful situations where they can have their own 'wit, skills, and passion for peace' (Appadurai 1996a). The community members do, indeed, bring their own wit, skills and passion for peace in their own way, but in extreme cases, in order to keep their place at the fringe, they lose their humour and peace, replacing it with stoicism and a pessimistic attitude.

For waste pickers, and communities like them, their original, rural, position of landlessness and unemployment, alongside economic polarisation, prepares the ground for migration, which in turn leads to the emergence of insurgent non-citizens in opposition to real citizens. This is marginalisation in the urban context. All of the waste pickers in my ethnography (2011–13) complained about a total lack of identity cards, social entitlements, proof of address or dignity, and no government system in place to furnish them with the rights to which they are entitled as Indian citizens. The Calcutta Corporation contests this stance, purporting that the majority of the community does have a basic identity card, for example, Below Poverty Level cards and voter's cards in their villages, but the NGO staff refute this. Anyway, the waste pickers argue that such cards are completely useless without access to any proper banking facilities, hospitals or any other basic facilities (where identity cards are required). In fact they have no rights; whenever they begin to organise any movement demanding their rights, they are branded as criminals. The state does not adhere to the International Protocol, according to which it is bound to give education to every child until they are 14 years old. Ironically, instead of receiving education from the state, the waste picking children are forced to work in hazardous conditions. In this respect the waste picker community are not only excluded from social planning, architecture, government and social structure, but also from any mainstream cultural and religious planning. They are, essentially, rejected by all quarters of society. They fail to cross the threshold of the aesthetic and cultural aspects of the city, and advancements in communication technology and concepts of virtual reality through computers and the internet are as foreign to them as modern loans and banking systems.

Job profile of the waste pickers

By anyone's standards, the waste pickers do not have proper jobs. Some of them hold the view that proper jobs are boring; the mainstream parallel is that the waste pickers are not competent to do them. Either way, the community members steal recyclable rubbish from the main dumping ground and other bins in Calcutta and maintain a façade that they are extremely afraid of the state and police. After receiving regular bribes, the police take care only that the waste pickers steal garbage in a quiet and inoffensive manner. Other elites from mainstream society take a different, very harsh, view of the waste pickers' occupation. Dr Rajendraprasad Sharma, an associate professor at the Indian Institute of Foreign Trade, believes this informal recycling sector is not efficient. Dr Sharma prefers the formal sector for waste management because it cares for the environment, whereas the waste pickers are, he says, disorganised, motivated by money and livelihood, and insensitive towards the environment. Many times I have heard it claimed that if the government/corporate sector/NGOs became involved in the business of waste picking on a formal basis, the people of the current waste picking community could receive uniforms, and be trained and well paid. If the government provided the funds, there could be a public–private partnership, and with a fleet of vehicles the business would run more successfully. Moreover, the waste pickers would no longer be marginalised; their lives and the city, in turn, would improve. On the other hand, one of my key informants appreciates the local wisdom and entrepreneurship of the waste picker community. He says that these people, apart from working as waste pickers, actually fulfil important roles as domestic help, vegetable sellers and at times engage in sex work under the cover of beauty parlours. Outwardly positive, it ultimately appears that the entrepreneurial capacity of the waste pickers induces a greediness that prompts their corruption. Nowadays the waste pickers can accumulate wealth, which in consequence makes them consumerists. They bribe local criminals in order to survive in their fledgling businesses and are soon trapped inside another vicious cycle of greed, corruption and increasingly superficial activities. From all angles, then, the waste pickers are 'stuck'. They will never come forward to be trained, for instance, at the local small-scale spice factory set up by the local NGO but will continue to exist as waste pickers. Waste picking is profitable. The community tells the NGO that if they can earn €2–3 per day picking up waste, they will never choose to earn 20 cents per day in the factory, or similar, even if the nature of the work seems more respectable in the eyes of the mainstream society. This is an ongoing complaint of the management staff of the NGO.

This in itself leads to another issue, in that the role of the NGO is frequently reported – and observed in my ethnography – as problematic. Its representatives do not dare to act as witnesses for the waste pickers or to speak up about the unfair acts inflicted on them as a marginalised community. If the waste picking community did not possess its unique skill of segregation and entrepreneurship, it would have perished from starvation. Alternatively, the waste pickers lose their social war when they neglect to label unfair acts by the police and NGO representatives 'social murder' and do not accuse the mainstream/elite/state of perpetually perpetrating this crime on them. The lenient and liberal NGO secretary, Mr Alamgir, comments that the waste pickers are wrong never to raise their voices. There are some exceptions (see pp. 42–3, 53–6, 63, 66–7 and 101–2 for the case study of Johra, Sabjan and Hannan); however, these are negligible and are more usually among the retailers to whom the waste pickers primarily sell their waste enabling them (the retailers) to form the link between the waste pickers and the recycling units. These retailers are also the networking agents between the waste pickers' illegal life and the state/mainstream society. I will return to the relationship between the waste pickers and the retailers later on in this chapter, and in Chapter 4.

Case studies

For three months between October and December 2011, in my role as researcher, I had the opportunity to become closely acquainted with several members of the waste picking community from the fringe areas of Calcutta. Nazma; her daughters, Seema, Rina; Phulmoni, her son; son-in-law Sohail and granddaughter took me inside their familial socio-cultural life and I witnessed their striving, entrepreneurship, sorrow and joy from very close quarters.

Nazma, the mother figure, and the son-in-law, Sohail, are the primary protagonists who offered alternative perspectives on life – grievances and achievements – as waste pickers. Nazma highlighted how, from a young age, she has built up this profession that she struggles to maintain through hard labour, in spite of her ill health (she has tuberculosis) and being abandoned by her husband. Nazma blames her son-in-law for failing to support the family despite his receiving a great deal of help from her: she believes that if Sohail proved himself a better worker, they could progress their business and promote themselves as retailers. Nazma complains that Sohail has an absurd kind of freedom from anxiety and immerses himself in gambling, drug addiction and alcohol. Even Nazma's children (including her young son who studies and lives in an Islamic boarding school) hate Sohail for his undisciplined nature, and tend to leave him to his own fate.

Sohail, on the other hand, expresses a deep resentment towards his mother-in-law – for 'exploiting him and turning him into a slave'. Together, they go out at between 3 and 4 am to rummage through the roadside bins and visit the Dhapa Dumping Ground (Calcutta's main rubbish dump). They work under the most unhygienic conditions, without proper shoes, clothing or gloves. Nazma regrets her family's misfortune and often asks herself, 'When will happiness come to our home?' Between them Nazma and Sohail earn about 1,200 rupees (€15) per week by collecting waste and selling it to retailers. They also collect fuel from the surrounding trees. Nazma is proud that they are so efficient at stealing fuel from other houses in the city that they never have to buy any for their cooking.

Waste pickers like Nazma and Sohail experience significant tension when dealing with the retailers, but the retailers, in a position to bargain easily with the community and retain their own prices, simply laugh at any argument. Therefore, the waste pickers, Nazma says, aim to keep them in a good mood: 'In general we have good relations, sometimes the relations turn sour and the retailers become angry. But on the days when the retailers smile that means they are agreeing with me in terms of prices.' In so saying, Nazma demonstrates her immense confidence in her negotiation skills. She narrates her dealings with her retailer, with whom she has dealt for a long time. She says, 'I try to charm my retailer to make him smile and do good business.'

A second family from Field Area I is headed up by Hamida, another female waste picker. She goes to pick up rubbish with her son, Md Shahrukh (14 years old) while her three daughters, Tabassum Khatoon (13 years), Neha Khatoon (12 years) and Tamanna Parveen (8 years), all work from home cutting rubber for rubber recycling units. Only the youngest one, Tamanna, goes to the non-formal school. Hamida has another son, Md Shohaib (ten years), who is also supposed to attend but in reality he goes to work with his brother and mother – although Hamida publicly denies allowing him to do such hazardous work. Hamida and Shahrukh, together with Shohaib, go out in the middle of the night to pick up garbage. Shohaib told me about the lanes and by-lanes of Calcutta that he has been taken through: Jin Mosque, the Black Dog Top, Mollapara, Sapgachhi. The waste pickers are not allowed in the main streets after dawn, but sometimes they cannot escape police harassment wherever they go, and they regularly have to pay them bribes. The family collects some expensive metals, metallic wires, glass items, steel cups, iron, plastic of varying quality (black, white and other colours), aluminium utensils, shoes for themselves, plastic containers, dairy packets (made of thick plastic), carton boards and expensive plastic cables – literally whatever recyclable material they can find. Back home, the sisters cut recycled rubber straps to make rubber sleepers; there is no time for a break or to play.

Members of a third group: Kala, Hannan and Johra Bibi, are exceptional waste pickers and differ from those like Nazma, Sohail and Hamida. Kala, Hannan and Johra dream big and have ambitions to become entrepreneurs or retailers and establish their own businesses. They are determined to reach the next level of retailers, who are able to deal with the non-formal recycling units directly. Although there is evidence of success for the luckier and more industrious workers, Kala has not yet fulfilled his dream, and probably never will, although he continues to try hard. He explained to me, 'Didi (elder sister) I am poor, I tried to be a big man but I failed.' Johra and Hannan's story is more positive. They have faced many hurdles but remained undeterred, continuing to put in hard labour and convincing their immediate colleagues to keep their trust and faith in them. Taking up all sorts of precautions and welfare schemes, to retain their co-employees/waste pickers, they have eventually managed to fulfil their dream of establishing an independent business with mechanised vans and even a lorry. Hannan and Johra are successful because of their ability to negotiate, innovate and ignore their frustration and negative losses. For the last 23 years, together they have taken many risks, and worked intensely without looking back at their past misfortunes. In contrast, Kala has been too easily frustrated by the lower prices he received from their retailers, especially in the initial period. His feeling of frustration held him back then, and he has remained an ordinary waste picker, only really developing fantasies of escaping his misfortune.

Johra, Hannan, Kala and their retailer peers are all aware that their profession is illegal; they are very clear about this fact, but they add, 'We are investing our honest labour. We are not doing any dacoit or robbery.' They see themselves as doing what they can to overcome humiliating situations created by the mainstream society when the mainstream society/state/elites harass and malign them. The community is simply building up its own tactics and contingencies to proceed with their business and break the stereotype of their anarchist position. Like the lower waste pickers, they are not exempt from harassment – at night the local petty criminals roam the settlements asking for money. Johra does her tricks and says her husband will call them and may pay them the sum. The goons go away. If Hannan does not pay the large sum of €220, he may well be beaten or kidnapped, so he promises to pay but never does because Johra protests that she and her family are not prepared to accede to a criminal gang. She even suggests calling the police. He is afraid and cautions her, but she is confident of being able to soften their aggressors. She says, 'Let the goons come and I will sort them out.' The husband feels extremely vulnerable and scolds his wife, 'What will you do? At the most you will quarrel and shout at them.' Johra claims that she is used to dealing with such goons, prompting the practical Hannan to retort,

> Please do not use your brain so much. Our power is nothing in comparison to the combination of the power of the police and the goons. They can burn down all our waste, all our business then everything will be plain and flat. So we are weak to them and it's been like this since the very beginning. It is the simple thing that big fish like them will eat us (the small fish) up.

The mainstream – comprising both petty criminals and the police and state – however, is not successful in eating them up, as the waste pickers are ready with tactics to tacitly resist. They prioritise things in their own way, which is misunderstood by outsiders.

Johra is a striking exception in the waste picker and retailer communities. After committing to Hannan, she continuously innovated in order to move their waste picking business into the higher level of retailing plastic. They waged an economic war with another waste picker, their son-in-law, in terms of transport. The son-in-law was supposed to provide them with his own transport in order to gain entry to Johra and Hannan's business. However, he always failed to meet deadlines and could not satisfy the vision and motto of the entrepreneurial couple. The couple decided to take out a big loan from a money-lender and purchased a lorry to carry their load of plastic recyclables, costing them €140 in repayments each month. Thus, in due course, the relationship between the couple and their son-in-law fell apart and he left their daughter, even after receiving a new flat with a huge dowry from the retailers.

One of the most significant, and very distinct, relationships in the community, then, is between the waste pickers and the waste retailers – something I have alluded to several times already. The constant ideological battle between the two groups, by its nature, never concludes. It gives rise to a number of questions, not least whether the waste pickers routinely move from one retailer to another, as they become irritated by the individual retailer's 'stinginess' (which is specifically associated with the refusal of the rich to help the poor) and greediness? (Scott 2009). I have observed the retailers becoming increasingly calculating in money matters, and the waste pickers are adamant they are less and less inclined towards charity – even towards their own poorer kin – referring to the 'old days' when retailers readily offered aid. Waste pickers and retailers, alike, agree that mutual cooperation and help is becoming rare, and both parties complain about this phenomenon. Under such circumstances, the waste pickers assert they are becoming deprived of their employment, tenancies, loans, charity and suitable feasts. Yet they will not join the Association of Waste Pickers organised by the NGO. Instead they remain with their long-time retailers, believing that somehow they will come through (with loans) in a crisis.

There is ambiguity about who is doing the greater favour for whom (Scott 1985). The retailers believe that the waste pickers should feel themselves fortunate to be in work, and so should acknowledge their fortune through their indebtedness. The retailers can allow themselves a pat on the back for helping the marginal population, even though the rents for the community may be high and the workload heavy. Therefore, the meaning of help can be equated with social weight, and the recipients' dependence is created according to their need. It has always been clear that aid is expected to flow in one direction (from the relatively well off to the needy), an expectation best demonstrated in the astonished anger of the waste picker community when the norm is violated. Is this a sign of shamelessness on their part? The waste pickers praise those owners/retailers who are modest and help the poor, and reproach those who do not follow this obligation of charity – accusing them of not fearing God. They say that the retailers are clever; they calculate and watch their money, implying that most are arrogant, proud and conceited, and thus they place the waste pickers outside the main resource area. In turn, the community is accused and criticised by the rich owners and retailers; something which happens most frequently when they fail to show appropriate gratitude through deference, small services, loyalty or social support, and ask for charity as their right. Retailers dislike attempts to negotiate pricing; they want full control over price and time of payment. The waste pickers who violate these expectations, for example, by trying to settle the wages before starting their work (perhaps because of previous negative experiences) are seen as cunning and calculating. Poor waste pickers, who refuse to work or who accept work and fail to appear, fall into a similar category of uncooperative and proud. According to the wealthy owners, a good waste picker who comes to sell his waste to a retailer should not only take any work at any wage, he should also be loyal and deferential. This equates to a minor ideological struggle over the social control of poor waste pickers. Deference and loyal service are necessary for the marginalised individual to qualify as 'good', but these 'good' marginalised people are highly criticised by their peers who do not wish to be 'good' (Scott 1985). Within these broad confines, both rich retailers and poor waste pickers have developed working strategies designed to devise normative principles that serve their mutual interests. The retailers, whose interests are directly threatened by the values of the waste pickers, attempt to bend their principles to minimise their obligations, place themselves in the most favourable light and trim back their ceremonial and charitable burdens. They try to project an image of themselves as living modestly, even suggesting they can barely make ends meet. They understate and downplay their economic comfort as a kind of conceit. In turn, the waste pickers adopt a similar strategy, emphasising their great poverty. Still, it remains that whenever a poor waste picker manages to eat and drink, whenever he or she is seen in new clothes or shoes, buying a cheap, almost rotten fish meal, or going by bus to visit relatives, this cry of poverty is to be a lie. The poor waste pickers always describe the retailers as rich, but they never slander them publicly or anywhere they might be overheard – so the garbage retailers again control the public opinion board.

I quickly learned that the economic gap between the rich retailers and the marginal waste pickers varies dramatically depending on one's point of view. From the perspective of the rich retailers, the gap is quite small; they themselves are barely getting by, while those (waste pickers) who claim to be destitute are actually doing well. As seen by the poor waste pickers, the gap is enormous; the rich owners are extremely wealthy and they themselves are poor indeed. On balance, it is more likely that where a few privileged owners monopolise the garbage collection units and income, the poor live from hand to mouth and are without any prospect, and generosity from the retailers' end is 'rare and insignificant' (Scott 1985).

Retailers, in attempting to minimise inequalities, also minimise their obligations to provide work and loans. It is very difficult to study power relations when the powerless are often forced to adopt a strategic pose in the presence of the 'powerful'. Both the powerful and the powerless take an interest in overdramatising their reputation as poor and resource-less. Not everything can be taken at face value, and yet, in the light of my ethnography (2011–13), it would be short-sighted on my part to consider 'tactics' as the whole story. All the 'contradictions, tensions, and immanent possibilities' should be understood. In this regard, dramatisation can be explained by reading between the lines of both the 'hidden transcripts' of the powerful people and the subordinate groups respectively – it is all about escaping their respective obligations to lend their own resources as aid (material resources from the powerful retailers and working capacity from the subordinate community), (Scott 1990, 2009). Subordination, or marginalisation, can be justified by the subordinated when it is taken outside the 'power-laden situations', for example, when the waste pickers' 'rumours, gossips, folk-tales, songs, gestures, jokes' are used as 'vehicles by which … they insinuate a critique of power while hiding behind their anonymity'. These patterns of disguise are globally referenced as an ideological insubordination of the subordinate community people.

By examining the multi-faceted social ties between the waste pickers and the retailers, I am deliberately emphasising the moral fabric of reciprocity, mutual rights and obligations. This fabric may give the community its social force and cultural rights; however, scepticism is warranted. Within the whole process of exchange, the goods and services given between the two groups are based on 'differing needs'. The real reciprocation that goes on includes the retailer's protection of the waste pickers and provision of material resources; the waste pickers are expected to reciprocate with their labour and loyalty. Even within a closely observed ethnography, it is not possible to measure the moral tone of such reciprocation, which is mainly marked by various ceremonies of ritual kinship or other symbolic ties on the retailer's part. This reciprocation can be interpreted as the authoritarian obligations that create the main configuration of justice behind the inequalities that determine 'the normative basis of power' (Scott, 1976: 181).

There is no question that the waste pickers' exclusion has political overtones. Occasionally they are pressured, for example by the NGOs, to become socially and politically incorporated into the state system. It is a pressure that provokes a variety of responses. Some waste pickers form loose attachments to the state or local elites, via club people and politicians, but at the same time try to defend their autonomy. This creates a strange and amorphous situation of 'engagement and disengagement with state and with mainstream society' (Scott 2009). Most community members, though, take up strategies to make themselves invisible and unattractive. They seek out their own no-man's land and continually move to that zone, one inaccessible to the state. In this way, the waste pickers are not bothered further by a state that may try to 'civilise them' or give them 'useful membership' to an alien (mainstream) society. As such, they 'betray civilisation' (Scott 2009). Their informal habitat becomes a refuge for criminals (mainly drug addicts and peddlers) and an escape route for tax-evading subjects. Overall, as a political location – outside the state but adjacent to it – these marginalised people represent a permanent defiance of central authority. But it is not that simple. In certain ways, the waste pickers do conform to accepted values – either for their own convenience or to cement their 'invisibility'. Although their social and cultural organisation, governance structures and legends all bear strong traces of state-evading or state-distancing practices, once the community settles down, its members learn the local dialect, try to marry locally and may bribe the local police for their minimal protection (Scott 2009).

Although much of the waste picker community's exclusion from the mainstream can be described as ideological marginality, it would be mistaken of me to ignore their specific expressions of distinctiveness and opposition. In Chapter 1, I acknowledged that which Scott calls the remote spaces of the marginalised people, 'places of refuge' and Appadurai calls a 'no-man's land'. This no-man's land, this narrow zone of refuge, has come to be known as the 'outlaw corridor' (Scott 2009: 133), a place of retreat for marooned communities, or a 'state resistant social space forged in conscious response and opposition to subordination' (Scott, 2009: 134). My ethnography reveals that the waste picker community settlements can be seen as a reformulation of the members' culture and religious practices. These may differ to the mainstream and within their own community: different factions of Field Areas I and II maintain linguistic, historical and ritualistic differences, for example, in terms of ethnic self-identification, kinship practices, burial and marriage rites, housing styles and subsistence practices. Usually illiterate, the waste pickers become involved in an oral history and culture which represents a 'more comprehensive rejection of states and permanent hierarchies' demonstrating their flexibility and spontaneity in creating their own culture and histories (Scott 2009: 177). Further, it shows that they do not have their own 'shrines, anthems and monuments'; they lack stories of their origins and are referred to as 'people without history' by the neighbouring mainstream.

This book claims that as the political control of members of the marginalised community weakens, their cultural influence regarding the state and mainstream society weakens too. Over the period of my ethnography, I clearly observed the occurrence of abrupt cultural and religious changes as friction increased between waste pickers and the retailers/owners. It is the community's relative ease of movement that suffers when there is a decline in their social and cultural integration with the elite/mainstream society and the retailers. However, it is equally clear that the waste picker community may well choose its social autonomy to attain a kind of freedom, even at the cost of material and cultural deprivation. In choosing to avoid incorporation into, and appropriation by, the state, it moves towards simpler, smaller and more scattered units and moves away from any collective action, becoming simply 'small aggregates of households'. Still, because of their lifestyles, the waste pickers remain coded as 'barbarians', 'primitive' and 'backward' by both the local elites and broader mainstream society. In summary: their choice of location, shelter pattern and occupation can be interpreted as 'social and historical choices' in terms of their own positioning of themselves vis-à-vis the state and other local elites/mainstream among whom they live (Scott 2009).

Education, and socialisation in general, is a further hugely significant case in point. Mainstream society stigmatises the waste pickers as non-members of accepted religious and political organisations. It regards those who evade the state as a failed or alien population unsuitable for any cultural advancement, and compels them to transition into a more civilised way of life. Thus, while the waste picker community has been left behind culturally and materially, the progressive section of mainstream society (for example, NGOs) equally believes it can be made into the object of development efforts to 'integrate them into sociocultural and economic life' through education and other training projects (Scott 2009: 128).

During my fieldwork with the waste pickers of Calcutta, I observed that marginalised people, who leave the realm of the state, are repelled by the state or become anti-state, frequently lack the conviction or motivation to access education or send their children to school. Even if they are invited by an agency to become involved in an alternative profession or non-formal education, the waste picker community commonly refuses; perhaps such lack of formality will not result in a 'proper' job. With regards to participating in training programmes, the waste pickers are unmotivated and do not demonstrate the same degree of entrepreneurial skill as when it comes to their waste picking, segregation and recycling.

When the government or an NGO arranges training in vocational skills or offers non-formal education, the waste pickers are impatient – in general, they desire instant gratification (products or money) from their endeavours, whereas education, formal or informal, takes patience and concentration.

The time of the waste picker children is not free from economic necessity, a precondition for the initial accumulation of education; they are sent out waste picking from the middle of the night until noon, and hence lack the time and energy to concentrate on school. If I revert (see Chapter 2), momentarily, to Bourdieu (1989) who links education directly with the investor personally investing in cultural assimilation and the time it takes, then due to their ideological marginalisation and occupational impurity, the waste pickers have neither the capacity for the required level of assimilation to elite culture, nor enough time to invest in education. Even if they have money, they lose the capacity to access educational capital as they lack legitimacy. Due to the foundation of a divided/biased society, they cannot access the economic and cultural means to prolong their children's education, which could have proven useful, even for their own occupation. That aside, it's true that both corporation and government schools mostly reject children from waste picking families anyway. The procedure of admission alone always entails hassle and complications, which causes the children to suffer – and their parents use this difficulty as an excuse not to enrol their children. This way they can blame the system and absolve themselves as being irresponsible parents. Children can still gain admission to the schools with NGO help and support but then those enrolled suffer mistreatment and unhappiness because of their waste picker identities. Both the parents and the NGO staff highlight a number of predicaments, which are ruthless in nature and debar the children from accessing education in the future. First, the children cannot collect money for their library fees, clothes and development fees. Such costs arise even though government education is supposed to be completely free. Second, the school authorities should provide children with healthy and hygienic food. In reality school meals have a very poor level of nutrition and are not at all healthy or hygienic. In order to avoid such circumstances in the mainstream schools, children try to persuade their parents to send them to the NGO's non-formal schools. These non-formal schools do not provide a good standard of education, but they try to maintain the children's respect and dignity. Next, the non-formal education, which the children of the waste picking community receive, lacks a proper uniform syllabus and appropriately trained teachers, alongside little to no record keeping of these children's' activities and development. In addition, the non-formal education centres of the NGO do not have basic facilities like drinking water and toilets. And finally, the non-formal schools do not avail of the opportunity to provide these most marginalised children with more training on collecting waste from mainstream corporate houses and multi-storey buildings; for example, how to behave in real life situations, how to dress properly, some basic management skills – without these basics, what is the point of education?

Ms Nath, the education and health supervisor of the NGO, is pessimistic about the waste picker community in terms of education. She reports that the parents never pay attention to children's education. Even if the children get some time to devote to literacy programmes, the parents will not encourage them because they believe education does not equate with income generation. Ms Nath reiterates how their waste picking occupation discourages them from pursuing any kind of education. The project for the waste pickers run by the NGO T-SHED containing a component of education has failed to convince these people that education can broaden their minds, enable them to create culture and may give them alternative livelihood options in the long-term. A total of 60 per cent of students drop out of primary school, starkly aware of the huge disparity between them and their mainstream classmates. Parents do not provide children with lunch and basic educational materials: 'While the other children are eating, we are not eating,' and 'While others have their items, we do not have the required educational items,' the waste picker children complain. They quickly become demoralised and drop out. In my quantitative findings, of children who attend the non-formal schools run by the NGOs, only two or three have passed the formal board examination; one waste picker boy, alone, opted for secondary education; he too became a drug addict after a while, and one young man already in that level did pass his Higher Secondary Examination.

Another professional, Ms Khatoon (one of my field colleagues), raises a vital question about why the NGO's non-formal educational system fails and the children leave school so early to return to waste picking. What is the root of this extreme lack of motivation? She suggests that the NGOs are not united in their mission to advocate adequately and lobby the government on behalf of the waste picker community. The strong network that could have been built up over the last 15 years is absent from Calcutta. Ms Chowdhury, also an NGO staff member, explained to me that this is not the case in other cities like Patna, Ahmedabad and Pune, where the situation of the waste picker community has changed and they are experiencing better living conditions. The waste pickers in the urban context of Calcutta remain depressed, dissatisfied and distrustful. The NGO (acting on the project to assist the waste pickers) is mostly concerned for the value systems of the children, who are exposed to pessimistic and negative attitudes through their parents and neighbourhood. As parents are keen to employ their children as waste pickers – to boost earnings – the retention of them in primary schools is difficult and high school education is almost out of the question.

All that said, it is worth noting how my research demonstrates a small but potential difference in attitudes (not attainment; dropout rates are similar as yet) to education between Field Areas I and II. The waste pickers from Field Area II are statistically more willing to receive education than their counterparts in Area I, and some boys and girls are even beginning to receive small stipends from government schools to continue their formal education. The NGO supports them too, and the NGO teacher is quite proud that their support has influenced the children to gain admission to the formal schools in the locality. Some of the younger children are – cautiously – even obtaining good examination grades.

It is evident that by rejecting formal education, the waste pickers become even more critical of the state/mainstream. They cannot endure the fixed pattern of stigmatisation or their negative labelling by mainstream society, so they hide their resistance and differences in order to avoid this backlash. As I described in Chapter 2, the waste pickers generally demonstrate tacit resistance; they rarely openly attack, criticise or pose any threat to the elites. Instead they take up strategies of non-participation, including covert nagging or grumbling, to trample both the reputations of the elite/mainstream society and the NGOs.

I have to conclude that the high level of non-participation in state education or even in non-formal education (provided by NGOs) among the waste picker children proves both their spiritual dilapidation and the bias of public policies concerning marginalised areas. The community's seclusion from mainstream/elite society is translated in the children as a corrosion of the self and a denial of state education. Socio-cultural/ideological marginalisation is evidently harmful; it fractures the will of these children and their parents to participate in any mainstream activities, and ultimately highlights the problems of moral deterioration, dysfunctional institutions and conflicts in their neighbourhood. This predicament gives rise either to the waste picker community's oblivion, or sensitivity to and avoidance of the role of the state as a stratifying and classifying agency (Wacquant 2010a). This has a powerful impact on their social, cultural and other symbolic (religious and ritualistic) practices. My ethnography (2011–13) demonstrates how the community is apathetic about self-improvement; making sacrifices and investing time for education is alien. The community, and especially its children, are placed inside a vicious cycle of economic necessity and ideological marginalisation. As such, the waste picker community and the NGOs have failed each other dismally.

4 Silent defiance and subtle negotiation

Marginalised people, like those who comprise the waste picker community, face 'multiple deprivation and destitution' (Auyero, 2011). Yet, through their efficient negotiation and engagements with different stakeholders (NGOs, retailers, club leaders, club members, mainstream housing complexes, corporate firms and charity organisations), the waste pickers in my ethnography do create a better understanding of ideological marginalisation – which converges in both fruitful and failed negotiation themes. In this chapter, I will address 'points of exchange' between the various faculties, and deconstruct the clash between the non-formal and formal markets as well as patron–client relationships and ideological marginalisation. I have, of course, already touched on the way the waste pickers subvert mainstream notions. After being uprooted from their agricultural bases, the waste pickers struggle through the job of segregating recyclables as best they can. On balance, they are happy to work as waste pickers – even given the unfair wages, the low financial value of waste, and price negotiation, none of which satisfy them mentally or physically. Mainstream society, generally represented by the state and police, shows little concern towards them; keeping their ego intact at the expense of the waste pickers means they thrust continuous misery onto them. Waste pickers like Nazma, Hamida, Husna, and Sohail (introduced in Chapter 3) see themselves as amid social warfare. Their houses are under siege as elites shamelessly demand bribes and plunder them under the guise of obeying the law. Yet, the state never feels it has failed these waste pickers in terms of social welfare; it simply questions how the community can continue to bear the fabric of marginalisation.

Kala, a waste picker/retailer whom I met as he relaxed at his shelter at the Park Circus squatter settlement, explained to me how the waste pickers divide their work and social areas between themselves. They allocate a few streets for specific waste pickers, and the Dhapa Dumping Ground is used as a common general area for segregation. They consider these areas as their cheque, and their skill in segregation and observation is the pen they use to write and sign the cheque.

Waste pickers Kala, Sohail, Azad and Abdu – all young males – share the same qualities and powers and they have the same interest in making merry after work. Their tacit agreement is that each keeps to his own side of the squatter settlement and they meet in a common space where they gamble, play cards and plan evening visits to sex workers and ways to feed their addictions. Female waste pickers never join in this merry-making; they have families to care for, household chores and television as their leisure activities. Women like Nazma, Hamida, Ayesha Bibi, Asma Bewa, Saira Bibi and Ameena Bewa passively share the brutal indifference of mainstream society. They are isolated, occasionally attending the focus group discussions and meetings called by the NGOs regarding their businesses and health or educational issues relating to their children and families. The women sacrifice themselves as much as the men are self-seeking. As a result, the project coordinator and the health supervisor of the NGO Tiljala SHED (also referred to locally as T-SHED) observes that the atmosphere of the waste pickers' community is not cohesive and that they suffer from the unfeeling isolation of each in his/her private interest. The State Conservancy representative and the NGO management express the same view that it is 'the more repellent and offensive the more of these individuals are crowded together within a limited space'.

Certainly, the waste pickers, especially the women and the children, confided in me their misery and endurance of 'social warfare' whenever they attend to receive treatment or give birth at a state health care centre, or when they wish to enrol in minimal formal schools like corporation schools. The battle continues when they go to fetch water from nearby slums. Despite this, it is quite clear to me, through interviews with the state and NGO representatives, that the authorities always stick to their indifference and hard egotism. The women and the children are afraid to speak out or to participate in the programmes offered to them by the NGOs or any state project. The men, if more vocal, are not heard. During my ethnography, a murder restricted the male waste pickers from their everyday gambling and card playing. The men repeatedly denied any involvement in the incident, even while the police entered and ransacked each man's shelter under the guise of the reciprocal protection of the law. Throughout, Kala, Sohail and their friends continued to stress their innocence. This is but one example of how the police openly and shamelessly wages a social war on the waste pickers. The police, along with state representatives, continually project the idea that the waste pickers' isolation comes from their narrow, self-seeking principles. The crux of the ideological marginalisation or socio-cultural warfare is the direct and indirect control of socio-cultural and religious resources and their production by the state and the mainstream/elites. This is the sole weapon with which this socio-cultural and religious war can be waged against communities like the waste pickers.

Waste pickers like Nazma, Hamida and Sohail explain how they are forced to lead a life of panic. However well they defend and regulate their 'space' (shelter, leisure area, markets and transport pathways), they run the constant risk of being raided and/or evicted; their shelters, their materials and their businesses destroyed. In addition, this space is inherently vulnerable. When a fire gutted 400–500 shelters within an hour on one April day, the entire existence of the community was in jeopardy. It underlined the community's need to set their space within wider relations of unequal power, resources and representations.

They had to seek help and support from the outside world – state, neighbouring international hotels and NGOs. All the waste pickers refer to their shelters inside the squatter settlements as 'luxurious apartments', yet they can be gutted in moments by fire or eviction. 'The harmony of "our luxurious apartments" can be short lived and shattered at any moment as on 5 April 2014,' says Hamida, an NGO non-formal school cleaner, as well as a waste picker. Even the most talked-about entrepreneurial couple, Hannan and Johra, lost not only their shelter but also all their savings and recyclable materials, including their waste pickers' portion of segregation, in that 2014 fire. The photographs from the devastated sites show how lost and helpless people became. For once, it levelled the waste pickers and the retailers involved.

The location of their space is important to the waste pickers. Sohail, Hamida and Husna prefer their shelters near their work places. Nazma, too, says, 'If we need to travel a lot before reaching the dumping ground then it will be complete loss. We chose to sleep very close to our work places.' Hamida adds,

> It is like a football match. Within these 7–8 hours in a day we must do all our business for the day. Beyond this time we are not allowed to do our business. This waste is like our ATM (automated teller machine), whenever we wish we can convert our waste to some money. Even we find precious materials like gold pieces, expensive metals and money in waste.

Johra uses the same words, stating that these as yet unknown, un-scavenged resources are for the waste pickers cash-equivalent. Hamida, Husna and Nazma appear almost in love with this resource of waste. They say, 'We may not have so many bottles as our retailers have but with so little we can do much.'

To be responsive and to survive in a competitive market like waste recycling, these waste pickers must coordinate with big retailers who have a strong network of suppliers from local grocery markets, retail chains and restaurants. Quite often the retailers are unhappy with the waste pickers as they can only supply a small collection, hampering bigger profits. These waste picker-cum-retailers believe they are the real players in the whole chain of non-formal recycling. Johra says,

> We are highly organised, apparently we may seem to be illegal professionals. We convince our employee waste pickers that this work seems to be the real hard work but it has its charm and it is sexy as in the end the waste materials are like gold. We lure the waste pickers by saying to them that it is more important to earn the money rather than building a shelter for them.

Johra takes pride in their easy loans to the waste pickers so that they can gain the upper hand over them. However, she and Hannan never display deep displeasure with their waste picking employees and they are preferred retailers for whom to work.

The solidarity of the waste pickers is built up through their gossip, character assassinations and public shunning of the retailers. In order to avoid drawing scorn upon themselves, they sometimes take up work even with reduced wages. Such short-term gains made by their constant adjustment may add to the anger of their fellow waste pickers, and could be referred to as the acceptable limits of self-seeking (Scott 1985). 'You can't cut your friends' is a unity dreaded by the retailers. The waste picker who crosses this limit is no longer respected by his waste picker friends and neighbours. Loyalty to a retailer is not so highly prized. Husna, Kausar Mallik and Ayesha Bibi, Sabra Begum and Arjina Bibi all complain to me that although they try to stick to one retailer for a long time, they are forced to move to another 'when the retailer cheats regularly and does not keep promises made during the bargaining process'. Ayesha Bibi was shocked when she found out that her retailer was hard and stern and refused even an extra penny for her well-being. Arjina left for another retailer to receive a fairer deal, and more opportunities, in order to achieve her dream of a better shelter. Ayesha comments that the retailers certainly take advantage of their weaker position. She affirms, 'We are here to gulp double-edged threats and exploitation from the Calcutta Municipal Corporation (CMC, responsible for civic infrastructure and administration), the police and the retailers.' The police, she adds, who beat people like her and burn their waste. As a united community, the waste pickers are critical of the corruption among the police (arguing that they themselves are not corrupt. Rather, the waste pickers see themselves as honestly earning money through hard labour, whereas the police earn money through coercion). When the uniforms come, waste pickers like Soleman, Chhad, Sabra and Sabjan have to run or else pay a large bribe. Others, such as Nazma, Hamida, and Sohail and his friends, have no time for the police but blame the state for their situation: they feel it is not doing justice to waste pickers' efforts to segregate recyclables to accomplish recycling.

To recap, then, daily, the waste pickers' lives are ones of facing coercion from the retailers, insulting and disrespectful attitudes from the police, and life-threatening events like evictions and destructive fires. And yet, at grassroots level, this is not the worst aspect; that is reserved for the daily challenges of their waste picking routine. These waste pickers risk their bodies through exposure to dirt and infection, to bites from insects, rats, snakes, scorpions and dogs. They exist in a climate of justifiable fear. Currently lacking any realistic possibility of directly and collectively redressing their situation, they have little choice but to adjust as best they can to their circumstances – despite deploring their loss of business and harbouring deep animosity towards the clique that dominates their local politics and entrepreneurship. They have no holiday from their mundane work, nor time to build or enjoy a decent socio-cultural life.

Case studies: everyday life, their food, health hazards and hygiene

It is no mean feat when participants in my ethnography, like Soleman Mollah, Chhad Banu Bibi, Sabra Begum and Sabjan Bibi, remain optimistically on the lookout for opportunities to upgrade their business. Such waste pickers have been headlined as 'backstreet entrepreneurs' in the BBC television programme *Welcome to India* (episode II, 2012), and it is Johra's life that really proves the truth of this label. Johra first became involved in the waste business of glass and plastic with her husband, Hannan, when she was in her teens, almost 30 years ago. She describes how they cut down the jungles at Topsia and Park Circus and built up the community squatter settlements. They put their lives into this business; they took big risks, faced large hurdles and have succeeded as retailers. Although they fight, she says, they live like a community. Retailers like Johra humorously refer to their shelters as luxurious apartments, and Hamida, the waste picker and the NGO cleaner, concurs with a smile, 'We live on unclaimed land. We don't need fans and air condition as we have our own down-choked polluted canals. The air comes from the canals. OK, see how I am putting on the air condition machine.' With which she just rolls up the plastic sheet that forms both door and window. Yes, it was amusing in the moment, and I could appreciate her grim humour when turgid air blew in, carrying a foul smell from the choked canal.

Shortly after this, Johra, too, invited me to visit her shelter. She takes real pride in the small toilet inside – a unique feature in a community reliant on makeshift toilets or Shulabh (low cost) pay-and-use toilets. She said,

> Come, and let me show you my world. I believe in self-made businessmen. I represent one. I eat whatever I make and I enjoy whatever I create. I have shown the world of waste and recycling what I can do even being a woman. I am a retailer in partnership with my husband Hannan.

Johra's employees and other waste pickers in the community regard the couple as true entrepreneurs, and almost all of the waste pickers I met during my ethnography do at least some business with Johra and Hannan. Some waste pickers, like Husna and Ayesha Bibi, even refuse to go into business or save with the NGO association for waste pickers as they feel more obliged to do business with the couple. Johra and Hannan have not only become big retailers, but they represent the zenith of the dream in the world of waste. Johra explains how the retailers, along with the waste pickers, mix some other materials with their plastic bottles for larger profits. They make a huge spherical bundle of 100 kilograms of plastic bottles to sell. The BBC (2012) reported that 60 per cent of the plastic in Calcutta is recycled by these informal marginalised people, an even larger proportion than in the UK. To continue in the profession, the motto of the waste pickers is to see waste as a gold mine, and the retailers think big. Combined, they achieve. As Johra says, 'We go for ship metal scraps even. Waste pickers bring only smaller metal scraps. But those smaller portions of metallic scraps are huge contributions towards this business.'

After spending time with Johra and Hamida, what struck me most significantly was how mainstream society still insists on calling these strong and resourceful women – and their male counterparts – 'non-citizens'. At the time of writing, the 2011 Census should have included the waste picker community, but the government does not count them as citizens or intend to give them any official identity. Although these marginalised people segregate waste more or less suitably – and the government itself is not carrying out any other appropriate segregation of mainstream garbage – the waste pickers receive no state recognition. Community member Sohail regrets they are only used by the mainstream society for useless work and crimes. For example, they are used to make up a crowd in an election campaign or meeting, to quarrel and pick fights with enemies of the political party which the community people support, to cast false votes or be manipulated to work at a cheap rate. They are even used to connect the mafia police and political leaders; all without even basic police protection from violence. Husna Begum, from the Park Circus area and another backstreet entrepreneur, angrily agrees that beyond their being used for political gimmicks or as cadres, political parties never offer the waste pickers facilities like banking or proper tenancy. After the 2014 fire broke out and destroyed all their possessions, I called on some of the waste pickers; among them was Husna. She just broke down: 'Why has this happened to us, Didi? We know about so many illegal matters of the mainstream professions too. They never get punished but as we are completely marginalised we lose everything.' At Park Circus, Husna Begum vividly narrated to me,

> Didi, sometimes CMC people and police come to our liquor and drug dens to have free booze and drugs and in exchange they give us secret news that the CMC people are coming to carry out evictions at Topsia and Park Circus.

Husna and their community do not get anxious as they are used to such news, but at Park Circus on the night of 5 April 2014 the warning did not reach them; Husna, Johra, Hannan, Kala and others could not gather their materials to escape before the fire broke out. In the aftermath, Husna wept like a baby and said, 'All our belongings have been reduced to a jumbled mess.'

The elite/mainstream society remains under its long-held impression that the waste pickers have 'foul language' in their blood; it goes some way to justifying the state's dismissive attitude. Drunkenness, sexual irregularities, brutality and disregard for the rights of property are the chief crimes with which the waste picker community is charged. This is not without substance, but the state fails to recognise this is far more the reaction to marginalisation, than the cause of it. That the waste pickers drink heavily is to be expected, especially when their earnings are paid and work stops somewhat earlier than usual – what else are they do? Where else can they go? When almost the whole community of waste pickers pours from its own poor quarters into the main alleys, it is inevitable that gambling, drinking and addiction are rife. This is one thing I have never seen first-hand; I have never been to their dwelling places on such an evening because the community warned me against it as a matter of personal safety, stating that if I did so I would face a sea of people staggering about, incoherent, and have to step over others lying in the gutter. I would see, they said, the same scene repeated over and over. And when their money is spent, the drunkards go to the nearest gambling or addiction or booze den, of which there are plenty in the area, and spend whatever they still possess. From the vast amount the community spends on intoxicating liquor each year the ensuing impact may be readily imagined: the deterioration in external conditions, the frightful shattering of mental and physical health, and the ruin of domestic relations. Sexual licence is endemic; this follows with relentless logic from the position of a marginalised class left to itself, with no means to make fitting use of its freedom. The state/mainstream/elites have left the waste picking community only these base pleasures, while imposing upon it a multitude of hardships. The consequence is that the waste picking community, to get something from life, concentrates its whole energy upon these enjoyments (gambling, drinking and sexual licence), carrying them to excess and surrendering to them. Women like Nazma and Hamida admit to using foul language without thought. Irritated by any disagreement, they quickly become intolerant; quarrelling with their neighbours, and scolding their own children by using slang. Should we be surprised? When humans are placed under conditions that appeal to the brute, what remains to them but to succumb to utter brutality? When the education of a community is neglected and they possess no security, there is little motivation to attain a common respectability or to sacrifice the pleasure or relief of the moment.

There are too many heart-breaking tales reflecting the vulnerability of young children who need protection against these negative anti-social practices. The story of Marijan, a mother who used to run a country liquor business (dismantled by the police 18 months ago) parallel to her waste picking, is a case in point. Her son, who helped her to run the liquor business, was still very young when he started to drink. The health supervisor who told me the story was visually angry that this boy, who was so intelligent, could never become literate or achieve any potential through such a profession. Sumita, a teacher from the NGO, narrates another sad incident, of Fatema Khatoon, a 16-year-old waste picker, who died of cancer recently. Her nephew has a hole in his heart and needs an operation. He was given a date for the surgery from the hospital but was unable to attend as his parents and relatives were all busy with Fatema's death. Because of the community's isolation from public institutions (which means it is excluded from the redistribution of basic economic needs and deprived of socio-cultural resources) these children – Fatema and her nephew – lost their opportunities of health and social welfare. Ultimately, their existence is marked by social and cultural monotony, leading to 'social closure and spatial relegation' (Wacquant 2008: 5) and cultural domination by the opposition. In summary, I might say that the results of this urban marginalisation I witnessed reflect the insufficient attention of the biased state towards the waste pickers. The chronic unrest of the community further incapacitates the state, which refuses to find solutions and thus increases the economic hardship of the waste pickers. Worse, the incapacity of the state triggers the social dissolution and cultural dishonour of these people. With their increasing civic alienation from their rights, they pose a serious threat to the institution of citizenship.

The domestic life of the waste pickers of Calcutta deserves further exploration because despite inappropriate behaviours and endemic vices, it would be wrong to suggest that family life does not exist but it is complex and erratic. In a comfortless, ill-furnished and filthy house, often neither rain-tight nor warm, with a foul odour filling overcrowded rooms, domestic comfort is impossible. The male waste picker works the whole day through, as do the wife and elder children; they meet in the night and morning only, the males apparently only doing so to receive home-cooked food. In the evenings, the male waste pickers meet up because of the perpetual temptation to drink. What family life is possible under such conditions? Yet the waste picking community cannot escape from the family and must live in the family. The consequence is a succession of family troubles and domestic quarrels, which are demoralising for parents and children alike. Male neglect of all domestic duties, and of the children especially, is only too common among the waste picking people. And yet the children growing up in this way, amid these demoralising influences, are expected to turn out good and moral. The requirements placed by the state/mainstream/elites upon the waste pickers are naïve. To prevent the 'superfluous' from multiplying, and 'demoralised' parents from influencing their children, families are broken up.

Health supervisor Ms Nath of Tiljala SHED says the waste pickers almost seem not to love each other. Parents appear to lack the natural love for their children and, in turn, the children lack the usual respect and love for their parents. Their intimacy or bonding with each other is low. This loveless situation continues in a repetitive cycle. The younger generation are stoic in nature; they never receive any respect, love or affection, so they also forget to develop the faculties to express these feelings themselves. When the NGO workers try to intervene they have to invest a lot of affection, otherwise the community people are just not accessible. It is a very difficult task and even after 14–15 years' work with this community, the progress is slow. The NGO workers try to arrange meetings and other necessary workshops concentrating on life-saving skills, but the waste pickers tend instead towards violent and abusive behaviour to get their own way. In Field Area I, Nazma and Hamida's opinion is that children should be removed from this kind of environment – where they only receive beatings and listen to strong, abusive language from their parents, neighbourhood and peer groups. Both women are concerned that if the children are continuously parties to such behaviour and language, they will be unable to concentrate on their education or any other training programmes.

On a more prosaic level, the waste pickers' food, health and hygiene featured strongly in my ethnography. Without exception, the families with whom I spent time are forced to eat poor quality food cooked in an unhygienic way – something I observed many times over. Their diet of boiled aubergine, rice and potatoes with some black cumin (kala zeera), garlic and onions, is cooked inside their only room, which means the smoke from the cooking fuel of coal and raw wood is suffocating but they must endure it. Seema, the eldest daughter of Nazma from Field Area I, spoke to me directly about their food habits. It is her belief that the food eaten during pregnancy is healthy, and they do try to follow such a diet generally; however, a lack of understanding of 'healthy' food or preparation is problematic. When Nazma bought a cheap chicken from the market for the engagement party of her second daughter, she herself wanted to cut the chicken in the halal style. The chicken was cut and prepared without any nod to hygiene; the blood was not washed off properly and the feathers not fully removed from the skin. It was cooked by Seema with rice and some vegetables, and it was cheap – the whole dinner for 15 persons cost about 350 rupees (€5), and they had left-overs. However, there was no refrigerator to preserve left-over food so either they ate the stale, gone-off food the next day or they threw it away. The family understands that its food is of poor quality, but still they prefer home-made food to that bought from outside, which would have cost them 20 times more money and brought little satisfaction. (The next day they informed me that the engagement party, and the food, were successful and they were happy about the whole affair. The marriage was scheduled for 2012.) Likewise, Tabassum, the eldest daughter (aged 13) of Hamida from Field Area I, also cooks food for her family. They buy some oily bread and eat it with fries (the oil is very cheap) and some boiled vegetables, which are not fresh (gathered from left-overs when the market closes) but are quite affordable. When they cook for lunch, they keep the same food for dinner as well. It is winter-time, so the food does not go off like it does in the summer.

The families make genuine attempts to maintain shelters to the best of their abilities. Seema, Nazma's daughter, cleans their room (10 ft by 10 ft) in which all seven family members live together; some of the family sleep on the bed and some underneath it. Nazma spreads clean paper mats for her prayers and namaz. Before the prayers she tries to wash herself, her son and her granddaughter. However, her attempts to wash are severely limited by water scarcity. Before their prayers, Rasul, her son, asks for a freshly washed shirt and pyjama suit – he attends a Madrasa, where he has learned that during prayers he should wear clean clothes – which Nazma can rarely provide. The little boy understands this, and together they pray sincerely and read a part of their religious text. There is no question in my mind that the waste pickers wish to remain neat and clean like most of mainstream society, but this acute water crisis is a constant challenge. They must collect water from distant places – after 4 pm and only after the local people have taken their share. They do not have any specific space for their bathing, washing and excretion – Nazma's granddaughter habitually urinates just beside their drinking water cans – and although nowadays, as they have money, they may visit pay-and-use toilets on the roadside, this expense increases their living costs. All the girls and boys of the waste picking community appear dirty and wear unwashed clothes. Kashmira, an NGO worker, confirms that, 'The community people always look unclean and dirty with films of dust,' but she questions whether this happens due to lack of water or the waste pickers' attitude towards cleanliness. On a visit to the non-formal school she asked two students why they had not taken their baths before attending school. The children protested that, 'We have taken shower properly.' Did they? Or do they feel shy about admitting that they do not have sufficient water for bathing? Their shoes, Kashmira reported, were always tattered, and they preferred to walk barefoot. Privately, to me, Kashmira suggested that the children look the same whether they shower or not. It was a comment and general attitude, I admitted to finding insensitive, especially as she went on to report that whenever the community do go to take water from the slum area, they are driven away and called thieves by the slum dwellers. Of course, they flee from the insulting situation. On rare occasions, a few of them will steal from the slum households and the entire waste picking community is then branded 'thief'. Quite often the community people face severe clashes with the slum people, and these incidents mainly occur in relation to water for bathing/washing and drinking. They face similar fights with slum people for using the toilets.

The most acute general health crises of the community have slowly begun to reduce. Previously, the waste pickers were frequent sufferers of severe diarrhoea, influenza and malaria. Nowadays, due to the intervention of the NGO, the acuteness and the frequency of disease has definitely declined. Family planning awareness has increased, too. However, the waste pickers are impatient; they always try to get quick results and are non-compliant – they are disinclined to observe correct dosages and complete a full course of medicine, so suffer longer and develop negative reactions. They are least concerned about their physical condition and the unhygienic and unhealthy environment in which they live and work means that they often have worms in their digestive system and contract jaundice easily. Respiratory and reproductive tract infections are the most common diseases among them. The number of tuberculosis patients has reduced, but again, this is affected by compliance – Arjina Bibi, the NGO's health volunteer as well a waste picker, had tuberculosis but because she went to the hospital regularly and consistently took her prescription, she was cured. The children are prone to colds, coughs and (including the grown-up boys) runny noses, but they and their parents are not too bothered about such infections.

Research shows that the city's public health care system is a 'non-system and is falling short and almost close to falling apart' (Wacquant 2008: 87) and state hospitals are grossly overburdened. Thus, the state health care system claims to lack the budget for the waste pickers and they rarely receive admission to public hospitals. Private health care providers also turn them down, charging high prices for treatment and refusing to treat them even in natal and pre-natal cases. Both public and private hospitals rid themselves of these marginal clients so as to avoid the financial burden they pose (Wacquant 2008: 87). The authorities justify this by saying that the marginalised people fail to 'supply proof of enrolment' (Wacquant 2008: 87). The NGO Tiljala SHED attempts to fill the gap. With the help of two doctors and five health workers, it regularly runs health camps for the waste picking families, especially for the children. The doctors treat regular diseases like influenza, intestine worms and common coughs and colds. For tougher diseases like tuberculosis, jaundice and sexually transmitted diseases, and pregnancy-related health check-ups, the doctors refer the waste pickers to the nearby health clinics and hospitals: National Medical College and

Nilratan Sarkar Hospital. This would be a good idea – if it weren't for the lack of encouragement from these state resources that I've mentioned above. Even these official referral check-ups tend to get disrupted as the state health clinics and the hospitals are negligent; refusing to treat the waste pickers or treating them rudely. Is it any wonder that the community does rely on the area hospitals or the local quacks instead? One story, from Hamida, tells how a surgeon negligently made a small hole in the bladder of a garbage collector patient's bladder. The callousness continued as the doctor gave him medicines that had passed their expiry date, and the patient was left suffering recurring infections. For once, the NGO investigated this incident and exposed the negligence to the outside world, but this does not happen enough. Hospitals are supposed to distribute free, good quality and effective medicines to the waste pickers but not regularly enough do they receive any medicines that can really cure their diseases.

I was with Shehnaz Begum (an NGO social worker and one of my field colleagues) inside the community of Topsia when an elderly woman called her and said, 'Baji (elder sister), Munni has given birth to a son in the middle of the night.' Shehnaz exclaimed, 'In the middle of the night! Has she been admitted to the hospital?' The elder woman smiled and said, 'Do not get upset Baji, I have cut the umbilical cord with a brand new sterilised blade; I got some clean cotton cloth and cleaned the baby. The baby is fine, enjoying his breast feed.' The elderly woman added that Munni did not receive proper treatment from the state-run local hospital and a bed for the delivery of the baby was not granted to her. I was surprised and Shehnaz was visibly angry that a birth could take place inside a shadowy, damp, unhygienic place in a big city like Calcutta, when any city hospital is bound to give a bed and necessary care to a pregnant woman. Shehnaz was unclear where the blame lies. Is the state too obstinate even to recognise the waste picker woman's labour pain or the woman too unaware of the risks posed to both herself and the baby? This is not an unusual story. Frequently women give birth to their children in their shelters. When a woman feels the pain of labour, she calls the neighbourhood midwife, and, like the elderly woman above, after sterilising a new blade, the midwife cuts the umbilical cord. They use some sort of clean cloth and hot water to wipe down the baby and the mother.

Ms Mita Nath (one of my field colleagues) emphasises another strain of risk: the occupational health hazards of the waste pickers. These hazards are partly of their own creation and suggest that they are careless about their lives. Waste pickers collect garbage from the main waste dumping grounds, where they sustain injuries and deep cuts from the various broken glasses, metals, nuts and bolts. Sometimes they get a tetanus injection, or as Nazma says, they more likely apply some herb, plant and root pastes and leave the infection as it is. One day Nazma got a deep wound, but she only bound the cut with a plant root so that no one could cast the evil eye on the injury. Only when her injury became dangerous and she was almost dying did she go to a proper private doctor – and spend a large amount of money. Otherwise Nazma, Hamida and their family members are among the many, already cited, who rely on quick visits to the cheap, private quacks.

Reflecting on the evidence above, there is a subtle but clear subtext: mainstream society deprives the waste pickers of welfare under the guise of negotiation. The state falsely claims it offers many schemes and facilities to the community, but the fact is that when the community attempts to access them, they are discouraged or prevented. This, I repeatedly observed during my research – and not solely in the arena of health. It related to hospital facilities, banking systems, education and state schemes for jobs. The waste picker community has repeatedly experienced the frustration of barriers and ultimate refusal of entry to facilities that are meant for them.

It would be realistic to wonder about the role of the NGO in relation to the health and welfare of the waste pickers. In theory, the NGO organises awareness campaigns on diseases and healthy practices, including: diarrhoea, malaria, washing hands, family planning, pre-and-post-natal care, children's immunisation, nutrition, child growth, breast feeding, gender issues, early marriage, physical and mental problems and contraception usage. The NGO arranges for a group of doctors to diagnose diseases free of cost, to distribute good quality medicine and to carry out de-worming. Tiljala SHED is the perfect example. It sounds good, except that it does not only fail those who need further referral to disinterested government facilities – these campaigns, the monitoring-referral services and clinics are almost entirely ignored by the waste picker community anyway. I observed the women occasionally availing of the services for themselves and their children, but the males were consistently reluctant to visit the NGO clinics, and never disclosed their symptoms or diseases. There is both a 'don't care' and an embarrassment factor, especially in relation to recurring sexually transmitted diseases (STDs). The NGO can only estimate that STDs are common among waste pickers and that, regardless, they fail to take the necessary precautions and refuse to go for proper treatment, appearing not to care about their physical symptoms.

For the waste pickers of Calcutta, it is even a fallacy that death is the great equaliser. On their deathbeds, they are not spared harassment. When they die there is no way of avoiding interment in the common graveyard under state authority. Mr Alamgir, one of my key field colleagues, gives a very forbidding picture of the community's deaths and funerals. In the case of the sudden death of any waste picker, doctors refuse to issue death certificates, saying that they were not involved in the person's treatment and so cannot certify the death, only through the intervention of the NGO – or huge bribes – can the family buy the death certificate. Even then, the doctors ask for witnesses from the mainstream society to confirm that the death was of natural causes, before providing the waste picker's family with the documentation. The doctors explain their behaviour by citing the case of a medical colleague who was harassed by police after stamping and signing a death certificate for a person whose death was later considered suspicious by the police. Mr Alamgir complains about this final lack of respect for waste pickers. Without the death certificate, the graveyard authorities will not allow the family to put soil on their land to bury the deceased. As a result, local small-time criminals have learned that this socially vulnerable group of people, at the most vulnerable time of their lives, can be extorted and blackmailed for large sums of money.

In terms of their general well-being and social welfare, the NGO management contend that the waste pickers prioritise their activities badly: the waste pickers do not earn any less than slum people, but unlike slum people they lack basic discipline. Future planning is completely absent in the waste pickers' lives. During all festivals, the younger generation of men hire videos and stereos to enjoy dancing. The males constantly consume alcohol or feed other addictions, which hampers the development of the community. On the other hand, women waste pickers like Nazma, Hamida, Husna, Sabjan and Johra (once upon a time also a waste picker) have all invested their money in their villages by buying land for agriculture and building homes, to enhance and develop their economic and social capital. Few male waste pickers invest so much in the future, those such as Hannan and Kala are exceptions. In regard to waste picker children, the NGO management regrets that the parents are largely irresponsible with regards to their children's well-being. Nowadays, as they have easy money, the waste picker community participates in every main festival, following the calendar of the slum people, retailers and the wholesalers. However, they are yet to spend this money on their children's nutrition, food and education – men like Sohail, Hamida's husband, are unwilling to allocate any expenditure to their children. Previously, even one or two years back, spending on education in terms of money and time was almost nil; the waste pickers imagined it was only for the mainstream. After a sustained effort from the NGO they are learning that education should be their first priority; key to a prestigious, dignified life, and as I described in Chapter 3, a few children are completing their secondary and higher secondary schooling. In other initiatives, the NGO is taking serious steps to establish a savings pattern among the community. It is trying all sorts of incentive measures, such as building up group savings and constructing self-help groups where the major component is saving for future investment. But, the representatives point out, their organisation has to be met at least half way by the waste pickers.

According to NGO staff members Ms Chowdhury and Ms Nath, 'In the long run the waste picker community people are cowards. They cannot come out of their decadence. They do not have the patience or creative mind to do any rebellion against this extreme, abusive and violent environment', and,

> They do not believe in each other; trust is in many ways out of their reach. So they are not united to build up any kind of movement or group activities. They are very poor in listening to other people. They fall in the trap to break into quarrels and fighting among each other very quickly and easily.

These statements reflect that the negotiation points between the community people and the NGO welfare schemes have failed miserably.

There is one work-based example of how poor the communication is between the two groups. NGO management told me that the NGO has established an association to create two rooms (in Field Area I and Field Area II) for stocking the refuse collections of the waste pickers. First, the waste pickers who become attached to these waste stocks register themselves as members of the association. Here they can store their wastes and segregate their collection and sell it to the retailers and the whole-sellers. The community people, under the supervision of NGO staff, save their money with their schemes. The community neighbourhood also participates in this association. However, the management is under the illusion that the majority of the waste pickers are with the NGO association, and the reality is different. The NGO staff told me the opposite; the majority of the waste pickers go to the non-formal retailers.

These practical examples partially answer the question of why the waste picker community remains outside of these NGO welfare schemes, which (unlike the mainstream facilities) are available specifically for them, but there is ideological reasoning too. My belief is that as marginalised people, the waste pickers are purposefully negligent of these projects through their own lack of motivation and stoicism to remain in their established position: out of reach of the mainstream society and the state. I understand there may also be outside influences guiding the waste pickers to avoid the welfare schemes. From my conversation with the mayor at the Council for Conservancy, it is clear that the state and local authority champion the view (see Chapter 3) that 'these people' should go back to their villages and not share urban resources like hospitals, schools and banks. In turn, the NGO services often are run on a shoe string or are temporary, which the waste pickers are programmed to consider failures from the outset; they will not bring any good to community lives. As such, it is unclear whether the waste pickers are avoiding such resources out of ignorance, or whether they are afraid of the frustration they know they will ultimately have to face if they do become involved.

In the waste pickers' view, they are caught between two (un)ethical and practical extremes. On one hand, the state representatives render them no service and maintain a superior, complacent attitude. On the other, mainstream organisations like NGOs and facets of the corporate sector offer charity that degrade those who take it. The waste pickers believe that this charity, in demanding that they are degraded and outcast, pushes them still deeper into the dust and obliterates their very claim to manhood. Then again, the state/mainstream/elites and the NGOs have different opinions as to how to 'deal with' the waste pickers; what is 'best' for them, and as such this leads to disagreements between the two official groups. For example, the NGO network organises a public hearing at the city town hall concerning the government's denial of the waste picker children's right to education. The network tries to put pressure on the government so that it will arrange an alternative system for these children – one that considers the structure of the school day, provides a proper building, electricity, educational tools and other equipment and ensures mid-day meals. The NGO staff is, however, doubtful about how long it will take for the state to implement such policies, and so they turn to the local 'club'. NGOs commonly enlist the help of the local club members when they find it difficult to solve any problem of the community, but even in this semi-official relationship, there is no love lost.

In this instance, only around 20 people belong to the club and the local venue is a small room with very few chairs, a table and some mats. Some of the waste pickers visit this club for their leisure time activities like playing cards and planning for future leisure activities. The club secretary of the neighbouring club inside the waste picker's community area, Topsia, confirms that the eagerness of the students to participate in their school-work has increased in the last ten years for two reasons: because the parents are taking more care and responsibility, and because of the mid-day meals provided by the NGO. Yet, the club members have manifold complaints about the NGO. They complain the NGO does not cook the food hygienically, and many children refuse to eat it. They complain the classroom environment is dirty, without chairs or mats. They complain that the space is not safe; the tiles of the roof are almost falling down and the drinking water in the school may be contaminated because the NGO staff collect the drinking water from a water purifier in a bucket which is not clean. As a result, the club members say, the children are uncomfortable and the NGO continuously avoids taking responsibility even when regularly alerted to the shortfalls. It is, thus, left to visitors and club members to try and rectify the situation. On their part, the NGO denies it has the money to carry out even routine work for the children's project, frequently declaring that the funding agency has stopped most of their funding. Although following this particular meeting the club members were satisfied with the quality of the education provided for the students, increasingly the NGO appears to fail even in these terms. It has, it is alleged, become more interested in corporate and house-donated waste than schooling – which the club members believe is because the waste recycling is very profitable. The NGO has, also, almost stopped holding meetings with the club members and the waste pickers' parents, neither does the NGO bother sufficiently to promote the Waste Pickers' Association. And the battle is ongoing, and everyone, especially the waste picker children, loses out.

Despite all of this, the club secretary insists that the club's own relationship with the waste pickers is positive, based on exchange and sharing. He and his club colleagues deny any harassment of the waste picking community. They claim that mainstream society 'likes the waste picking community and does not look at them as outsiders but as friends'. The club is Hindu, and as such, the secretary says, they invite the waste pickers to attend the Hindu festivals and, in turn, the waste pickers return the invitation whenever they throw parties, mainly during the Eid festivals. The club members say there is no discrimination during the holy occasions; everyone sits together to share the same food and have the same fun. According to the club members their help is never sought in relation to police harassment against the waste pickers. But whenever the community members are in trouble for stealing or anti-social behaviour, they come. Mr Sahu (the club leader) says that the waste pickers sometimes steal household items – inexpensive, good quality plastic – and others are heavy drinkers and consume drugs. Whenever these pastimes create trouble with friends and neighbours, the waste pickers run to the club members for advice and to pacify the situation. (As an aside, when asked about the impact of drug addiction, the club members say that they never allow a single addict into the NGO school area.)

In terms of work, the club secretary maintains a strong opinion on the relationship between waste pickers and retailers: it is generally a good one, assisted by club members' negotiation when required. Every day, he says, the waste gatherers and retailers must exchange money and waste in the waste recycling units, so neither party will ever harm the other, and neither do the recycling unit's owners ever insult the waste picker community. If they did, the waste pickers would boycott that specific owner. They argue that the waste pickers have a very successful market and are therefore never afraid of the retailers. However, the club members do identify a possible 'treachery' on the part of the waste pickers. Sometimes the waste pickers take advances from the retailers and then, with the loan in hand, go to other owners to sell their items – so they need not repay the loan money. At this point the owners do use abusive language to criticise the waste pickers. This insult works; the waste picker feels ashamed and returns to the previous retailer. The waste picker says, 'Sorry, elder brother. I am wrong. Please forgive me. I will never do this. Please cut my interest from the lower range.'

Significantly, the club secretary is highlighting another area of important negotiation between the waste pickers and the waste retailers. It is my contention that any relationship between the community and their retailers (and, indeed, the club) can be fair but is always fundamentally unequal. Although the waste pickers and the retailers live in a similar condition and environment, the retailers (see Chapter 3) never consider waste pickers for kinship or arrange marriages with the waste pickers' families. The reason for this formality is because the retailers consider the waste pickers to have a lower status, socially and economically – and they are the ones who give easy loans to the waste pickers whenever they need money. Waste pickers like Nazma, Hamida and Husna are aware that the retailers will never consider them equal and marriageable, but their relationship with the retailers still carries a bond, which has positive ramifications for their profession and earnings. The pickers may sometimes visit the retailers' houses for feasts, festivals and rituals, but the retailers never reciprocate by visiting the waste pickers' shelters. Before the pickers had television in their houses, they were welcome to go to a retailer's house to watch TV, but this is a kind of investment; it ensures that the picker's children continue the same business arrangement as their parents. Hannan, the retailer, practised this and, during a festival like Fateha-Dwazzam, Hannan still prepares biriyani and invites all his picker clients to share the food. Hannan is a Bihari Muslim from Canning, his wife, Johra Bibi, is a member of the women's organisation of the ruling party (previously CPI(M) and now Trinamool Congress). They both nurture a strong connection with the police, so they never worry about extortion. Hannan sustains his long-term business with the same waste pickers due to his patience, permanency and inclusive, empathetic attitude towards the community. This couple help the waste pickers during their marriages, funerals and crisis collections, they even offer jobs to children who lose their parents at an early age and support other retailers in conflict situations, including domestic ones. Recently Kauser, another retailer, was arrested after his wife complained at the police station. But Johra and other field women helped to get him released. Hannan's sense of justice and tremendous capacity for hard work have made him the preferred retailer in the locality.

Other waste retailers, such as Kadbanu, cannot maintain this level of constancy – sometimes succumbing to criminal extortion – but all of them try to give the standard rates to the waste pickers. It is standard practice for the good retailers to support their neighbours and kin during their desperate moments, for example, with loans and physical support and when they have to go to the hospital. At the same time, though, they do not have any faith in each other. They cannot build up a saving group or self-help group, whereas other communities are more successful in this regard. An unfortunate feature of their mistrust is that they never help other waste pickers if an attack comes from the outside. When the slum dwellers attack one of their members, they never come out of their shelter to defend their neighbours.

Referred to by the club secretary, an organisation called the Association of Waste Pickers, potentially a valuable self-help group, has been nominally run by the community under the guidance of the NGO for the past 15 years, but its official-sounding title is something of a misnomer. Here, male participation is extremely low. The ratio of the men to women is 1 : 10. The female waste pickers prefer to work with the association rather than individually, whereas the males do not want to lose control over their occupation and individual businesses. Unfortunately, the NGO has failed to initiate any ownership of this association among the waste pickers themselves. The community does not find this association a supportive entity or accept it as their resource exchange/sharing centre. In consequence this (huge, well-intentioned) effort by the NGO for the community is mostly wasted. Not a single exchange meeting is organised by the waste pickers, so in a way the waste pickers also lose the opportunity to exchange with the outside world or the wider mainstream society. In the self-help-groups it is ironic that only six members are waste pickers among the 50 local members who save regularly and carry out the programmes of development, unity and empathy with professional colleagues and the neighbourhood. Individually the waste pickers can understand profit very well, so it is confusing that they do not participate in group activities which may give them more benefits. It's likely that the low number of waste pickers in the self-help group, in comparison to other poor sections of the population, highlights a mode of protest against mainstream society. The waste pickers doubt whether the effort of the NGO is effectively catering to their values. Community members like Sohail, Nazma and Hamida say angrily that they receive little in the way of support, loans or other necessary materials from the association. They feel that a single storage space for 350 families is not sufficient, and they expect that they will not receive the necessary benefits and dignity.

As part of my ethnography (2011–13) I established a number of focus groups to invite discussion, primarily between the waste pickers and the NGO Tiljala

SHED. Some new and different stories, directly from the waste pickers' mouths, emerge through these focus group discussions (FGD). They may not give a full account of the waste pickers' lives, and they are endlessly contradictory, but they do support the contention that waste pickers can overcome challenges and supplement their lives.

Hasi Bibi, Chymoon Bibi, Litun Sheikh, Aynoor Seikh, Amirun Bibi, Asura Bibi and Aftoon Bewa spoke about a conference of waste pickers at Pune (a city in Maharashtra) in early 2012, which identified several areas in which the waste pickers of Calcutta fell behind their counterparts in Pune. First was the need for identity cards. With such documentation from the NGO they could go directly to the mainstream households and collect the recyclable waste – as is done in Pune – and they would be harassed, beaten up or arrested by the police for being without ID. Countering this, though, the NGO is sure that the waste pickers do have identity cards, or at least their voter's card, because they go back to their villages during election times. That aside, the waste pickers also discovered that those in Pune receive money, gloves, shoes and even transportation and replacement from the Maharashtra State Government. If the Maharashtra State delays the provision of these essentials, then the waste pickers stop working and the state comes under pressure to resume provision. Third, they noted that in Maharashtra the women waste pickers were self-sufficient and never depended on the male waste pickers, and finally, the Maharashtra State Government has even provided the waste pickers there with medical insurance. This would be unthinkable in Calcutta, West Bengal.

As a result of this discussion, the few Calcutta waste pickers who joined that day's meeting resolved to form some kind of unity to procure their rights from the state. This arises from the fact that waste pickers nowadays can see through the empty promises of the NGOs and the state. Both previously promised to secure community identity cards, some uniforms and recognition of their occupation via information about various state schemes for employment and insurance. Farzana, Monowara and Yasmin told me that nothing has been done by another FGD meeting on 10 June 2012. This time, the discussion mentioned a programme about unskilled labour that had been held on 10 and 11 May 2012, encouraging a movement against the abuses faced by the waste pickers. But only five of the community had attended.

On a separate occasion, the NGO workers tried to explain to Raju, Soleman, Sabra, Monoara, Chhad Banu and Putul the importance and utility of redeveloping the Waste Pickers' Association and saving schemes. The community could have a working, viable association, but it is dysfunctional not least because male waste pickers like Raju, Soleman and Kauser slide too easily into gambling, alcohol and other entertainments. The NGO workers, they say, try to inspire the waste pickers to address these alcohol-related problems, but without success.... After hearing this, it was the NGOs' failures that concerned most of the subsequent FGD. The NGOs previously promised fair prices in waste deals with the community, good saving schemes, vocational trainings and advocacy for the betterment of the community, none of which – again – they did, but neither did the waste picker community – again – take any initiative. The NGO says it has tried to create micro insurance and saving schemes with the waste pickers, but as they (say they) have no identity cards and fall within the migratory category they cannot be linked with the proper banking facilities.

Human Rights Day was on 10 December 2012, and at the specially planned FGD, the NGO workers explained the significance of human rights to the community people. The organisers then asked Arjina Bibi and others why they had not turned up at the councillor's office to discuss their water scarcity. They blankly answered that he has repeatedly rejected their appeals and they were sure that the councillor would never listen to them. The NGO workers tried to convince Hasi Bibi, Monoara Bibi and Soleman Bibi that as association members they would have opportunities to demand legal addresses, welfare schemes for unemployed youths and elderly people, and birth certificates. The NGO worker said,

> We will guide you to take the right path. You can follow this right path and can succeed if your community is unified. You must demand for your own respect. We know you have no basic amenities like toilets, sanitation, water and no legal documents. You can sort out all these through this association.

This whole situation seemed ironic, as waste pickers like Raju, Anwar, Husna and Monoara are aware that joining any association will not solve their problems, nor (from experience) will the NGO workers ever fully stand beside them – it is not possible for this feeble NGO (Tiljala SHED/T-SHED) to organise the community to demand their identity and food ration cards – so they do not have time to pursue such mirages. However, in these meetings, the waste pickers do behave differently. They are extremely dignified and Raju, Husna and Monoara's speech is emphatic, clear and not repetitive.

As this chapter has expanded, several voices of the NGO management and staff, the club leader and club members, waste pickers and the retailers have emerged. It is very clear that, while all have valid wishes and opinions, there is little cohesion, a lot of argument – and even more inertia. The NGO management tries to establish that they are doing their best to achieve the betterment of the waste pickers, but the waste pickers rarely respond appropriately to the facilities and education provided by the NGO. The NGO staff blame the waste pickers for their negligence and lack of motivation. In another Focus Group Discussion meeting, on 7 January 2013, the waste pickers explained that the police station never accepts their complaints about harassment – they are always called the thieves. No one in the mainstream/elite society even considers the waste pickers as proper human beings. Sheik Munna, Saira and others admit that they lack the unity and discipline to fight against such inhuman attitudes. The NGO workers tried to create leadership among them, but none of the above waste pickers was ready to be the leader. They would not agree to visit the police station to talk to the officer in charge about procuring water and sanitation. Korimon, Sheik Munna, Ajmeri and Saira are certain that the police officer in charge or the councillor would refuse them flatly and that their old spaces and basic amenity crisis would continue.

The chaotic nature of the emergent voices points to the fact that marginalisation, as endured by the waste pickers, is actually arising because of the state. It is the state that has failed altogether to deliver adequate support and welfare schemes. The research in this book demonstrates that the relationship between the waste pickers and the NGO, retailers and club members can be called a client–patron relationship. My ethnography further shows that the assumption of these relationships develops as a result of that dysfunctional state/elite. Patrons only operate when the state fails to provide the waste pickers with universal access to welfare resources. At such a juncture the patrons like the NGOs, club members and the local clubs emerge to take control of what access there is to the resources (Blok 1988; Holston 1989) but they are limited in what they can do. The NGO, running the project for the waste pickers, and the club, mediating between them, can create roles for themselves as arbitrators between the state/mainstream society and the waste pickers, but this ultimately benefits them rather than the waste pickers. As such, the patron–client relationship between the NGO and the waste pickers is clearly not working and has failed to give rise to an alternative system to the faltering democratic development of the state (Blok 1988; Holston 1989). The waste pickers' words reveal that although their encounters with the NGO are not unpleasant, the NGO cannot make their dreams of entrepreneurial activity and socio-cultural fulfilment become reality. Their unfulfilled ambitions, half-done household religious rituals and dreams of sacred spaces create a sense of intense regret about their lives. NGOs and other agencies like the state and mainstream/elite society fail to recreate an alternative space where the waste pickers can forget their own moral and material dislocation.

I have, however, revealed that although the patron–client relation has ultimately failed in terms of NGO activities, patron–client relations between the retailers and the waste pickers still function. The retailers are clever enough to understand the intricate policies of control over resources. They can attract the waste pickers and establish a long-term relationship with them through their sense of constancy, integrity and networking with mainstream politics and state apparatus, such as the police. The retailers help the waste pickers by intervening when there are problems like police harassment. These retailers are the only stakeholders, apart from the NGO, able to negotiate successfully with the waste pickers and create a position for them in the non-formal market of recycling. The NGOs utilise them to collect the recyclable waste from the mainstream/elite housing complexes and corporate firms for income-generating programmes. To gain recognition for the waste pickers, the NGO tries to find a practical solution and says it does give them informal identity cards for temporary periods. Thus the waste pickers find themselves less socio-culturally marginalised when they go to collect waste from housing complexes and corporate firms. According to the waste pickers, in spite of this and their ability to segregate waste positioning them in the non-formal market, their recognition is often suppressed by the dominant state and other elite/mainstream sectors.

Negotiation with mainstream

Interested in extending my ethnography to consider the interaction between other, different stakeholders and the waste pickers, and how the stakeholders react towards the community, I interviewed the managers of three corporate firms who are responsible for the donation of recyclable items to the Association of Waste Pickers run by the NGO. My first interview was with Mr Ravi Kumar Basu (senior manager, operations, and asset services) of CBRE South Asia Private Ltd. This company handles the waste management of companies that have no waste management policy, and as such meets environmental and health and safety needs. Those serviced basically donate paper, plastic, woods, metals, computers, chairs and tables and avoid donating hazardous and confidential items. Mr Basu told me that since the company's inception in 2002 it has been part of their policy to donate recyclable items to the waste pickers. He feels that the condition of the waste pickers is very pathetic and their deprived lives should be improved. However, speaking on behalf of companies he represents, he says they have limited time and money, and so can do very little for the community. When I asked him how close his connection with the waste pickers is, Mr Basu confessed he has only come into contact with them through television and the NGO. Individually he is in a helpless position; he wants to help this community but his corporate profession does not permit him.

My second interview was with Mr Nibir Kumar Tribedi, an assistant manager at the Facilities Management Group, working for Wipro Limited (DM block, Sector V, Salt Lake, Kolkata – 700091). I interviewed him on 16 January 2013. This company started to donate their waste to the NGO in 2004–5 and the company policy is to dispose of 90 per cent of the waste as a social responsibility. In particular they make certain that a minimal amount of waste goes to the ground – ideally no more than 10 per cent. They donate paper to Tiljala SHED. The company has a sewage treatment plant and they recycle and reuse their waste-water inside their campus. They also decompose food and garden waste as organic waste. To make the world 'gutter' free it is necessary to recycle as much waste as possible to make it usable once again, and Mr Tribedi believes the whole informal recycling system is quite good. He believes that the waste pickers are human beings who should have access to education and at least the minimum of amenities and facilities for their social life. More NGOs, government and corporate sectors should come forward to make the waste pickers' lives better, and new policies, rules and regulations incorporated to bring them into mainstream social life. Mr Tribedi admits he has no direct contact with these waste pickers; he only sometimes sees them doing their work, searching for plastic containers and bottles from the garbage dumping zones.

The third interview was with Dr Rajendra Prasad Sharma, an associate professor at the Indian Institute of Foreign Trade. This Deemed University in Calcutta started to donate waste to the NGO in June 2012 under an NGO-attached initiative called the Social Awareness Programme. This is a programme of management courses, not book-based, but a collaborative project with 20 other

NGOs – an initiative that helped me to carry out my fieldwork. The university's aim is to develop its students as socially-conscious and sensitive businessmen and women, and joining with the NGOs for welfare causes is part of this. The NGO motivated them to donate their waste, like damaged mats, carpets, cartons, newspapers, lamps, tubes and other glass, plastic and metallic items, for the benefit of the waste pickers. Mr Sharma has a high opinion of the waste pickers, believing they are compelled to do this job as they are uneducated, and are of great use in society: 'In a way they are cleaning the park where I go for my evening walk.' He believes that if the government/corporate sector/NGOs can get into this waste picking business on a formal basis, the community will get training, uniforms and be well paid. If the government contributes funds, there can be a public–private partnership. If the government provides vehicles, then the business will run more successfully. Moreover, then the waste pickers will not be marginalised and their lives, and ultimately the city, will be improved. When asked about his interaction with the waste pickers, Dr Sharma said, 'No, so far I have no direct contact with them. However, if T-SHED organises some interactive sessions with my students to do field work I am keen to do it. The session will bring about some transparency.' He said, 'We will come to know about the fate of the recyclables donated by us. Depending on this the institute can take bolder steps with the NGOs.'

The corporate stakeholders are all part of a formal market. They are liberal in their views about the position of the waste pickers, but at times they are insensitive in regard to the non-formal market system to which the waste pickers belong. The corporate stakeholders are judging, theoretically, the lives of the waste pickers and taking a benevolent stance towards them. However, their experience is derived from the formal market and does not allow them to encode the mechanism of the non-formal markets of the marginal people. Instead, they are prompted to regard the waste pickers as subordinates and dependents from the peripheral regions. It is obvious from corporate people's language that they can appreciate the waste pickers' economic marginalisation, but they are unable to grasp that at this juncture the waste pickers' cultural and religious marginalisation is more crucial in the creation and experience of dependency. These corporate individuals have both formal citizenship status, and rights which allow them to pursue their conception of a good life. Their status gives them power to ignore or suppress the similar pursuits of others, especially of those who are in marginalised situations (Marcus 1983). The state protects those who have formal and legal status at the expense of marginalised people in order to maintain the status quo. In return, the corporate stakeholders keep up their minimum responsibilities, which involve paying taxes or participating in the pacification of the marginalised people by donating their recyclable wastes through the NGO (Marcus 1983). In summary, these liberal corporate people think that they own a set of rights as legal citizens and they acknowledge the corresponding duties – in this case, the donation of wastes to the marginalised people.

If the corporate stakeholders have no personal or practical experience of the waste pickers as people, this lack is mutual. The waste pickers' daily lives are far more dependent on the NGOs, receiving regular aid from three or four organisations, including Tiljala SHED and Christian missionary charity Calcutta Samaritan. As well, they go to Kumbh and other Hindu fairs to beg. They leave no stone unturned, exploring all unskilled avenues to earn money, although it is quite peculiar that they depend on these hand-outs in spite of their own good income. Negotiation with any NGO is a complex matter for both the waste pickers and the organisation. The waste pickers understand that the NGOs receive huge amounts of money from international funding agencies for their development and welfare. They see that if they can instigate a competition between the NGOs their community will make a profit both materially and in terms of betterment. They literally blackmail the organisations, and sometimes they favour one organisation over the other. The NGOs are aware that their waste picker clients are clever and are playing tricks. During my fieldwork, Tiljala SHED wanted to talk to Calcutta Samaritan regarding the distribution of work, but Calcutta Samaritan was not responsive. Sumita, the NGO teacher, complains that 'Calcutta Samaritan is poaching T-SHED's children and families'. It helps on a small scale, such as giving the waste pickers rice cards to trade for their lunch of khichri, or during Christmas, on 22 December, doling out cheap woollen shawls, rice, lentils, biscuits, milk, cooking oil, cakes and oranges, but when serious issues arise (like community conflicts, marital disputes and police harassment) only Tiljala SHED works to resolve them. Sumita explains that T-SHED is the local organisation, so they have more powerful networks, and after working for the last 34 years in the same area, they have developed expertise in dealing with police and political harassment of the waste pickers. Tiljala SHED bears the cost of the waste pickers' education, medical and health care, marriage at the proper age and funeral costs. Calcutta Samaritan has only entered the community in the last two to three years. Sumita says: 'They never entered into these areas of crisis, but this year they are trying to attract the waste pickers by bribing them with good hot meals and medical camps.' Tiljala SHED is also seen to carry out more work on advocacy and lobbying state apparatus, such as the Conservancy Section, and, significantly, has given some of the community ID cards (although their availability remains disputed by some of the waste pickers). These, as we have discussed above, are coveted and can make a huge difference. A case in point is Jabbar Sheikh, a hard-working waste picker, whose wife is a domestic help. Their four children are getting a proper education in formal school. Jabbar does not take any addictive substances. They are very well organised and keep their shelter in good shape. Once he was given some recyclable items, which were materials from a criminal theft and he was harassed and arrested by the police on the Park Circus connector bridge. He was released after the real suspects were caught, but crucially he was able to show his identity card to the police. The police respected this card and it was instrumental in securing Jabbar's freedom.

Conclusion

The complex competition between these two NGOs reflects their mutual goal that the waste picker community be included in mainstream society. Both organisations are aware this will require long-term social movements by the community itself, parallel to advocacy and lobbying by the NGO Tiljala SHED. Yet, the marginalised waste pickers are devoid of the will to struggle. My ethnography (2011–13) demonstrates that the waste pickers have no intention of changing the nature of the existing socio-cultural supremacy of the mainstream/elite or the state. Further, they have no aim to change the negative opinions of the public/mainstream society, even under the influence of the NGOs (Holston 2008). They refuse to bend to the rules and regulations of mainstream society (see Chapter 2).

As service providers, the NGO staff and external NGO reviewer (international funding agency: Misereor, Germany) claim that any of their projects aimed at the waste picker community has too many components to be effective long-term. These components include: income generation, waste business with corporate houses and multi-storey buildings, health intervention, educational intervention and cultural intervention. As such, the NGOs have insufficient focus and measurable objectives and targets, and cannot meet their commitments. Despite this critical condition, the corporate houses have promised to donate huge quantities of recyclable materials to the project. In turn, the NGO, with the waste pickers in partnership, can then sell these to generate income. The NGO management claims that this proves how the NGO is at least partially-efficient in running the projects, although it is obvious that there are many gaps (clearly outlined in the audit report of funding agency Misereor, Germany, 2012). There are other agencies, such as housing complexes, corporations and small firms, sometimes empathetic towards the waste picker community. They donate huge quantities of recyclable items for income generation programmes and the development of the waste pickers. But in return, the larger society also receives benefits from the community in terms of waste segregation and recycling; it would not have been affordable for them to pay council tax for the recycling process. This is one of the major points of exchange and sharing between the waste pickers and wider society. However, this process of exchange still happens entirely through the NGO, and for the NGO, and so can be categorised as an artificial exchange or negotiation point.

In seeking an easy, cheap fix, the waste picker community is attracted by the neighbourhood Ponzi (chit-fund) scheme agents who take away their saved money and invest it elsewhere. In return, the waste pickers are supposed to receive interest along with their initial deposit if they wish to withdraw their funds. They deposit their money with these chit-funds for 12 months in expectation of gaining a high rate of interest and should then receive the money in a lump sum. It is, though, usually a scam; the waste pickers are generally cheated by the agents, who conveniently vanish from the neighbourhood. The NGOs try to stop this investment in the Ponzi schemes, but the waste pickers are lured by their accessibility and less authoritative nature – fewer rules and regulations – than even NGO schemes. The community reasons that if it is excluded from formal banks (due to lack of proper documentation; even their local councillors will not sign their papers as witnesses) what else can, and should, they do? They feel that developing group saving schemes or group businesses under the NGO umbrella leaves them at risk of being trapped inside the framework of a mainstream institution or authority. The waste pickers' trust in the conventional way of doing things is broken.

Here, I will conclude by saying that the process of exclusion from the regular institutions and economy of the mainstream society influences the waste pickers of Calcutta to become 'demoralised' (Wacquant 2008: 177) and to distrust the mainstream organisations and institutions. Such exclusion prohibits a collective movement for the community's rights, and adopts instead an 'individualistic ideology of achievement' (Wacquant 2008: 180). Perennial non-participation in the NGO-arranged education, health care system, saving schemes, self-help groups and other training programmes reflects the waste pickers' absence of community feeling, and they refuse to recognise the collective nature of their problem. The waste picking community from the 'symbolically spoiled zones' (Wacquant 2008: 197) experiences socio-cultural ostracisation from mainstream society on the one hand, and on the other, it negotiates with the stakeholder as far as possible for freedom from economic marginalisation. These negotiations give rise to a patron–client relationship indicating the failure of the state in tackling this marginal urban population.

5 Challenging social capital

Formulation and subversion

The ideological and economic marginalisation of the waste pickers is uncontested and clearly measurable: they are considered an eye sore to the 'normal global world' – the world comprising ATM machines, credit/debit cards, a well-defined banking system, huge mortgages and loans on consumerist products; the world of housing markets, cars, education, health care and stock markets. The waste picker community is not connected with computers, internet-related high-end gadgets and information, legalities and the judiciary. The state machinery daily closes all avenues to them for accessing shelter, tenancy, education, drinking water, medical health care and sanitation. They never receive protection from the police against anti-social people and politicians. Furthermore, the waste pickers have little resistance to amend their position. The evidence gathered during my fieldwork (2011–13) indicates that while the state and mainstream society leave them behind, it is also beneficial for the community to drag their heels; they will stick under the mainstream radar and both groups can continue to escape each other. The state uses manipulation to keep national resources out of the waste pickers' reach and, along with society, evades its duty to support them as citizens as per the Indian constitution. It is a two-way street however; as the community needs its freedom for their beneficial underground existence and the state/mainstream society requires sole ownership over national resources.

These basic observances demonstrate the marginalisation of a community that cannot envisage its inclusion within social networking of any kind, let alone possess any socio-cultural capital. It lives day to day, hand to mouth, without imagination or forward thinking. Bearing this in mind, and with reference to relevant contemporary theory alongside my ethnography (2011–13), this chapter considers the ideological marginalisation of the waste pickers of Calcutta in terms of their social capital, drawing on the experience of their regular life activities. The core of the discussion is how the community's struggle is rooted in the formulation, or subversion, of social capital. Consider first the words spoken by Mr Alamgir, the secretary of the NGO:

> I can guarantee that they (the waste pickers) never dream of any air-conditioned car, or living inside any posh apartment. They can at least dream about the 65 square metre shelters with the basic sanitation and safe

> drinking water – sharing with another 25 families. Unfortunately many don't even have that minimum dream. Our organisation tries to facilitate them to dream by giving them micro-finance, saving schemes and health schemes. We try to lobby with the government to stop forced eviction from their shelter.

When I asked him further about the waste pickers' idealism and dreams he started to laugh. He spoke of their very simple dreams; they are simply struggling to survive. Even if they dare to have dreams, they know these will never come true, but still, they do not want to face their own reality, constantly wishing instead to be inside the realm of their media-fuelled worlds or inside the fantasies created by their addictions. If anything, the current generation pays lip service to a desire to link themselves into civil society (through the NGOs) and beyond, that their children will get higher education, a good value system and become further established in society. In reality, the waste pickers don't do anything to disturb the status quo; they can't. Their mindset is locked in day to day survival and their pattern of consumerism reflects this. NGO observations, matching my own, confirm that male waste pickers spend the best part of their money on their addictions: chewable tobacco (mostly all men), alcohol (women too) and hard drugs (affecting fewer people). A great deal of money is also spent on religious and marriage festivals and the associated accessories like food, dresses and entertainment. For example, when Hasina, one of the community members, gave her son in marriage, she took almost €400 from the bride's family as dowry. This she spent, proudly, on food and drink for the reception guests. Aside from such special occasions, it remains that it is women who are mostly responsible for family expenditure. Having no time to cook their meals, except their dinner – in spite of the NGO's advice – the mothers give 20 cents to their children for breakfast, so the children eat unhealthy fatty food from outside or receive a charity lunch. The women pay for cooking fuel; mainly they use spare wood and other materials like waste leather and wood as their fuel. Women also pay for 'pay-and-use' toilets and bathrooms for the whole family, and they spend on childbirth, towards which the men do not contribute. In fact, the men are reported to use all the facilities the family can afford but without taking any responsibility for the family. Overall, the waste pickers place least financial importance on the education of their children, and they also spend very little money on medicines and health care.

Challenging social capital: formulation and subversion

My ethnography (2011–13) has already detailed the way the waste pickers tend to conduct their social (and economic) lives, and the evidence is that alcohol, and sometimes, drugs, play a central part, especially for the men. Some have admitted that they occasionally degrade themselves to sub-human levels once these substances have been consumed. At such times, is it possible that the affected waste pickers become stoics, and as such, completely disconnect themselves from both their own and mainstream society? The whole discussion is fraught with ironies. The joint secretary of the NGO provides an example:

> Yes they (the waste pickers) are celebrating nowadays the Eid, they are fasting during the Ramadan month. They participate in the religious functions. They will wear new cheap dresses. They will eat some meat and fish. But where is their real improvement? They are not getting any proper job.

He regrets that the community members do not complete their education or look for more mainstream work; they do not think beyond immediate gratification. The Mayor of the Conservancy Section stands with him. The mayor is also 'puzzled' as to why the waste pickers are so deeply involved in their profession and refuse other work. He does not have any direct contact with them, but he sometimes talks to them when they collect plastic from the vats. He explains how the Conservancy Section tried to give them night shelters in different parts of Calcutta, but the waste pickers have always refused, saying the shelters did not cater to their interests. Then – the real crux of the matter – the mayor goes on to contradict both himself and the joint secretary, saying, actually, (even if they were willing) it would be impossible to give the waste pickers jobs in the organised sector because there aren't any suitable for them, they are not ready to settle for any urban wage employment scheme, and are reluctant to do jobs procuring less remuneration than their present income.

I learned from the NGO staff that the mayor is highly critical of both waste pickers and NGOs, and he represents the norms of the mainstream society in stating that the waste pickers – a nuisance only – should either leave voluntarily or be removed from the city. Neither does he support the constructive activities of the NGOs, but fortunately he has no power to stop them. A further irony, then, is how the NGO management also tends to blame the waste pickers for their lack of planning – yet how can they plan without stability? The corporate donors only donate their recyclables because the NGO acts as a connecting link; they would not donate to the waste pickers directly. Their 'generosity' is dependent on the NGO; arguably, they would otherwise think of the community as criminals and thieves in the same way that mainstream society does.

At root, it is the vulnerability of the waste picker community that is to blame; it makes them permanently apprehensive and unable to think beyond the immediate. The waste pickers live on illegal land, at risk of eviction or forced relocation by the government and Railway Authorities, and living as such, their children face criminalised behaviour every day and are more likely to become drug addicts or drug dealers. Ironically – again – my NGO field colleague, Mr Alamgir, is highly critical of his own organisation for unintentionally perpetuating this vulnerability, but equally, their hands are tied. He believes that the philanthropic work of the NGOs is about 'fancy rights' (and schemes) not 'real, hard-core human rights' (and schemes). The NGO makes the waste pickers aware of the issues that lead to their marginalisation, but does not intervene to provide solutions; for example, they fail to adequately lobby government and do not question the harassment by the police. And herein lies the politics of mainstream society and the problem: if the NGO did ask the police to protect the waste pickers' families the police would simply harass the NGO instead and stop its activities. Mr Alamgir says, 'They will put us on the black list and will hinder our funding process.' Precluded from political work, NGOs are of limited use to the government anyway, as they cannot go to the waste picker community with political statements or activities. Still, the political parties and state representatives, like the police, simply take bribes from these marginalised people and, as mentioned above, expect their support. The waste pickers do not have any conventional political inclination and they do, always, depend on the ruling party; whenever called upon, they respond and join its rallies. This, of course, will be the same party mainly responsible for attacking them, but the waste pickers have no other option because they are only permitted to follow the ruling party and those clubs which also support it. Even when the party engages in criminal activities the waste picker leaders assist, and give shelter to, party workers.

It all goes to show an almost tangible culture of blame, not only towards the waste pickers but, internally, among and between the mainstream organisations themselves. Such is inherent in the government-organised child protection scheme too. The NGOs are very critical of this 'child line'; a representative claims that, 'these child lines are all eyewash. There is no sincerity, no sensitivity from the NGOs or from the government/political parties.' But the NGOs are tied once more: the government, police and the local mafia repeat the set norms that the NGOs should not empower the community. Their role is solely to perform welfare services; the giving of milk and bread, and at most, support education and healthcare.

Social resources (which define the social position of the community using them) comprise economic, cultural and social capital components. In turn, cultural capital exists in three forms: first, as adopted in primary childhood; second, in cultural articles; and third, in cultural institutions. It is expressed in terms of certificates, diplomas and examinations (Bourdieu 1983, 1984, 1986) and my ethnography (2011–13) provides information on each dimension. The waste picker children learn definite socio-cultural acts and concepts in their childhood. For example, they use overheard slang language, and they adapt to living without sanitation, hygienic practices or dress codes. At the same time, they internalise their profession of waste picking and social segregation. Next, the cultural articles of the community consist of television shows and cheap videos of Bollywood and Bengali films and songs. Third, institutional intervention in terms of culture is rare in this community. If the NGOs insist, they might watch educational programmes on television but the majority of the waste pickers are illiterate, and not attached to any formal institution that could provide them with certificates or diplomas.

Social capital is a resource more connected with group membership and social networks. 'The volume of social capital possessed by a given agent depends on the size of the network of connections that he can effectively mobilize' (Bourdieu 1986: 249). Membership of groups, and the social networks arising from membership, can be utilised to improve people's social position in a variety of different fields. Voluntary associations, trade unions and political parties are modern examples of embodiments of social capital. I have already reiterated how the waste pickers neither belong to any formal groups or clubs, nor are they involved in any social network. Rarely do they participate in any voluntary associations organised by the NGOs. The illegality of their profession precludes support from trade unions. Political parties only use them for crowd pulling and criminal activities. Differences in the control of social capital may explain why the same amount of economic and cultural capital can yield different degrees of benefit for different people, and social capital created by group membership multiplies the influence produced by other forms of capital (Bourdieu 1986; Coleman 1988). This alone is a convincing explanation for why the waste picker community lags behind in all spheres of economic, social and cultural capital.

My ethnography (2011–13) indicates that, at best, the 'successes' of the waste picker community are uneven. Households appear divided into losers and winners according to wider economic profits; at times they even fear one another, mindful of potential bullying by their neighbours. Those who participate in the association's waste collections benefit from cooperative economic success, but there are many who cannot access this limited resource. Despite a number of projects attempting to assist community development and build on supposedly existing social capital, it is clear that the NGOs, and other institutions aiming at community betterment, must rethink their models of support: 'Families should not be led into fragmented groups each distrustful of the other,' was another opinion expressed by the NGO's Mr Alamgir. NGO staff, volunteers and management conform to a stereotype, lacking creativity and innovation. They routinely adopt a softly-softly approach, providing only light education and healthcare; unwilling to risk the provision of training on human/workers' rights, or, as we've seen, lobbying the police and government. According to Mr Alamgir the staff are too casual, and are not well enough trained themselves, especially in key areas like child protection. They fail to revise or review their approach, follow-up and feedback is entirely missing from their programmes and there is an absence of result-based work. Neither is Mr Alamgir satisfied with the quantity-based work that is presently being carried out within the NGO: the children and adults attend and the programme ends. If this is the case, it begs the question already floated: wherein does any real gain from NGO services lie?

When examining the socio-cultural and ritualistic activities of the waste picker community in the context of social capital (including how far they deviate from, and subvert the concepts of, social capital theories), I originally intended to write about the resistance put up by the community. However, since the nature of resistance in such communities is highly complex and multi-layered, I believe it can be better explained by the theory of social capital as it appears in the work of Bourdieu (1983, 1986), Coleman (1988) and Putnam (1995, 2000). The quality of public life and the performance of social institutions and the representative state are powerfully influenced by the norms and networks of a community's civic engagement. Researchers in education, urban poverty, unemployment, the control of crime and drug abuse, and even health, have discovered how civic engagement and social connectedness produce results through mechanisms such as better schools, faster economic development, lower crime and a more effective state. For economic achievement, too, the community needs both social bonds and an understanding of the importance of this bonding and bridging process. My research highlights the influence of networks: interpersonal and inter-organisational networks that are the key for a successful community. This is particularly significant because the waste pickers clearly demonstrate the potential for negative, rather than positive, results with respect to the failure of these networks. The data I have collected during fieldwork shows that the community, within the framework of social capital, has failed to develop 'the tools and training that enhance individual productivity'. It has not become part of 'any social organisation such as networks, norms and social trust that facilitate coordination and cooperation for mutual benefit' (Putnam 1995: 2). It is not 'blessed with a substantial stock of social capital'. In the first place, networks of civic engagement foster sturdy norms of generalised reciprocity and encourage the emergence of social trust. Such networks facilitate co-ordination and communication, amplify reputations and thus allow dilemmas of collective action to be resolved. From my ethnography (2011–13) it is clear that the waste pickers' life and work does not encompass collective action and is not immersed in reciprocity and trust between neighbours and colleagues. When economic and socio-cultural negotiation is embedded in intense networks of social interaction, incentives for opportunities are reduced. At the same time, networks of civic engagement embody past successes in collaboration, which can serve as a cultural template for future collaboration. Finally, dense networks of interaction probably broaden the participant's sense of self, developing the 'I' into 'We'. This enhances the collective benefit.

The ethnography further highlights ambiguous results from different perspectives. The mainstream/elite/state report that the waste picker community's backward attitude restricts them to collaborating with their neighbours. The waste pickers' ghettoised life never gives them the required dense networks of interaction that could have broadened themselves, developing their 'I' into 'We'. The waste pickers do not understand the mutual benefit which can only come when their economic and socio-cultural negotiation is embedded in intense networks of social interaction. Hence, their incentives for opportunities are reduced. The social ties of the waste pickers are framed in common symbols, common retailers and, perhaps, common ideals, but not in one another. The theory of social capital argues that the existence of the association should act to increase social trust, but this is not always applicable. The waste pickers do not show trust in each other and therefore they cannot increase participation in the Association of Waste Pickers initiated by the NGO. In consequence, social connectedness does not always emerge from the same category (Putnam 1995). Another source of social connectedness is represented by non-profit organisation and non-profit service agencies – a third factor important to assessing social capital and civic engagement. Although support groups like the local NGOs and the local club are expanding into health care, education and other self-help services, the waste pickers, feeling marginalised, are not getting sufficiently involved and therefore not giving this potential the chance to flourish. The non-profit organisations cannot replace the role of traditional civic associations and cannot fulfil the needs the waste pickers have in the absence of their rural ties and social connectedness. They cannot substitute for real family or neighbourhood ties, or even friendships and any attachments to the NGOs lack life-long exchanges and commitment. Although the NGO staff and management proclaim that they are ready to offer broader community attachments, they try to preach to waste pickers about their social code of conduct instead of supporting them to retain their 'own binding capacity' (Putnam 1995). From the available data, my research concludes that social capital in the community has been eroded significantly, and from all possible angles, within the waste picker community. Any social connectedness gained through the NGO – according to community members – reflects only the weakest of obligations.

Likewise, my ethnography demonstrates how little trust the community people have in their neighbours, and, moreover, how much this continues to decrease. Since social trust is correlated with educational levels (Putnam 1995) and because the waste pickers' investment in education is negligible, the overall decline in social trust is even more obvious – even if the NGOs try to control the waste pickers' educational participation. Looking at Putnam's theory (1995), this trend of mistrust among the community people is explainable. Trends in social connectedness and civic engagement have assumed that all the forms of social capital are themselves coherently correlated across individuals. I have clearly observed that members of the association are more likely 'to participate in training and project programmes, to spend time with neighbours, to express social trust' (Putnam 1995: 8) than the non-members. This is evidence that social trust and civic engagements are strongly correlated. The greater the density of associated membership in a society, the more trusting its community people. Trust and engagement are the two facets of the same underlying factor: social capital. And one of the important reasons behind the decline in social capital is the significant increase of waste pickers' working hours and the growing involvement of women in their work (Putnam 2001). The time and energy left for activities that may build up social capital outside their working hours is consequently much reduced. However, the crucial point is that the engagement of women in the work force has not reduced their household chores; their husbands do not share the burden. Thus the workload of waste picker women has doubled. Conversely, the other reason behind the decline of social capital may be the technological transformation of leisure. Putnam: if 'there is reason to believe that deep-seated technological trends are radically privatising or individualising our use of leisure time and thus disrupting many opportunities for social capital formation' (1995: 9), the most obvious and probably the most powerful instrument of this revolution, in the waste picker community, is television. The women and the children are almost addicted to television and, whenever free, pass their days and nights watching it. This has done massive damage to social and educational building; they are uninterested in any other educational or cultural programmes organised by the NGO. Television offers private entertainment at the cost of the positive social externalities associated with their previous leisure forms. The same logic is applicable to the men's entertainment, also dependent on watching movies on videos/DVDs, and means this new, revolutionised virtual reality is ultimately isolating. As such, technology is driving a crisis between individual interests and the community's collective interests, and is hampering the production of social capital (Putnam 2000).

The extent of the crisis

We have already seen that the NGOs are unable to motivate the community to defer gratification and create their own socio-cultural capital. As an interim measure, the NGOs are now trying to generate social capital in the sense of mutual reciprocity: by encouraging the resolution of dilemmas of collective action, the broadening of social identities and an emphasis on associational life. The hope is that the waste pickers will discover their own structures of networks by default, enabling them to create their own appropriate social capital via a different means. However, it appears the NGO's approach is accompanied by growing intolerance and the erosion of traditional social capital. This contributes to the corruption and discrimination within the community caused by the failures of the state.

NGOs must urgently explore the depth of the failure of state policy. The existing social capital of the community is dealt a tremendous blow by the state's squatter clearance police, which ostensibly exists to renovate the physical capital of the state. As a result of this policy, the waste picker community has developed a feeling of increasing insecurity and acute distress, arguably causing a rise in illnesses, drug addiction and domestic violence towards women. This was once again proven when fire materially gutted the Park Circus community on 5 April 2014 and the waste pickers also lost most of their remaining social capital of trust and engagement. The resulting challenge was how both the NGO and the community might restore this capital. Perhaps the NGOs should force the democratic institutions to support the community in developing social connectedness, thus creating a slim opportunity to build up civic engagement and civic trust? The NGOs could work for state-provided social welfare, as promised in India's constitution. Certainly, instead of encouraging the strangling brand of philanthropy endorsed by the state, NGOs should guarantee the introduction of state-based altruism towards this community, enabling them to regain their trust and engagement with each other.

Fundamentally, the NGO management and the conservancy representatives – the latter most harshly – suggest the waste pickers are themselves to blame. Had they struggled through their hunger and stayed in their rural home places, they may have maintained good social capital. Indeed, the conservancy suggests the solution is for them to go back. But these are not answers. Rather, all quarters of society, starting with the community itself, should make an effort to foster bridging and bonding capacities. Social capital is far from homogenous; the NGOs and the state need to consider multiple dimensions of it, based on meaningful networks and reciprocity, for the waste pickers. The waste pickers' social connectedness, and therefore social capital, is enhanced through the incidents like visiting each other's home, and the frequency with which they volunteer or participate in, for example, their children's educational meetings. The very low average number of waste pickers who attend the meetings of the NGOs, clubs, association, self-help groups etc. in any one year is an example of a lack of this interconnectedness and reciprocity. Altruism, too, is linked with a strong social connectedness, especially true in relation to the retailers. The retailers who give more money, throw feasts for the community and have volunteered their time to accommodate and train the waste pickers in their businesses are the retailers who are most connected. However, it is still true that this connectedness is not without its own conditions. It is also related to the retailers' financial resources how well they are connected to social organisations, and how often they visit their nearby police station or local political party office.

The social forces that would like to demolish the welfare state have developed the concept of competence, which extends the ideas of social capital. 'The ideology of competence serves very well to justify an opposition which is rather like that between masters and slaves' (Bourdieu 2000: 42–3). On the one hand there are some citizens who have rare and overpaid capacities and activities, and then on the other side there are the marginalised people like the waste pickers condemned to borderline jobs or unemployment. This competency provides justification for the dominant group's privileges and is accepted by the dominated (Bourdieu, 2000b: 43). The structure of inequality is given ethical and intellectual justification at the same time with the help of the ideology of competence: 'The poor are not just immoral, alcoholic and degenerate, they are stupid, and they lack intelligence' (Bourdieu 2000: 43). The existence of an excluded and under-privileged group, with all the problems consequent upon this, is thus indirectly legitimised. This social consensus is hegemonic in nature. Consider the state as a fountain or super-agent of the symbolic violence that guarantees the system of dominant symbolic power – it does so with the help of a monopoly of symbolic classification and categorisation, especially in the educational system (Bourdieu 2000).

So, is the waste picker community in crisis? The NGO answer is 'yes', to which I would broadly agree, but according to the waste pickers it is not the whole truth. Both opinions are outlined and discussed throughout this text and retaining such different perspectives, as well as that of the state/elite/mainstream and representations of all stakeholders, has posed a tremendous real challenge. It is readily apparent, however, that after 16 years of their project with the waste pickers, the NGO itself has placed the community in perennial crisis. The NGO has – probably in order to save jobs and the project – always blamed its failure on the waste pickers themselves. The NGO complains that the community is non-cooperative when it comes to planned project work: that they will not engage with educational initiatives, cultural activities or with saving schemes, or the Association of Waste Pickers, and it is because of this that their crisis will never end. Perhaps the truth is that if this crisis is resolved, the NGO will lose this huge project and their jobs?

There is a complex balance of power between the mainstream/elite society/state and the waste picker community. The former do not acknowledge the contribution of the latter and the latter actively avoid their influence on the former. Here I have attempted to show specifically that the state and its allies' possession of power cannot connect with the community, nor can they impose their influence on the community. There is no relationship of dependence between the waste pickers and the state/mainstream/elites; the community as a whole is relatively independent in terms of its socio-cultural processes. The waste pickers, however, are bound to come under state power through 'disembodied abstract contracts' in which power mediates and changes the waste pickers' lives even though they position themselves in a zone of autonomy (Bourdieu 1989, 1990).

I think it is evident why the community fails to engage. Even after the 400–500 shelters were gutted by fire in April 2014, the state did not accept the urgency of their desperate situation and were not inclined to help – so, of course, the waste pickers lose the capacity to be concerned with abstract matters or intellectual pleasures offered by NGOs. Of course they postpone all activities related to the state, including healthcare or education. Of course they feel inferior, and so they use the hidden symbolic power of their own habitus to build up their own discipline and absorb the punishments arising from their rejection of anything formal. The only obligation the waste pickers maintain is to the waste retailers, who in their eyes constitute the single symbolic authority. The retailers represent and operate all economic functions for the community. In the long run this deviance from a system of obligations breaks both their socio-cultural ties with the culture and religious life of the mainstream/elite society, and their own kinship ties. And at times they might even determine to detach themselves from the retailers – to show their resistance. This behaviour can be analysed as moral absconding, a crisis of moral norms on the part of the waste pickers.

Most social scientists see community members as socialised and their actions as being governed by their specific social norms, rules and obligations. Action is described in a social context and the way it is shaped, constrained and redirected by the social context is explained inside the frame of the marginalised community. The alternative view is that the community member has his/her independent goal, and acts independently and wholly self-interestedly. If we follow the first view, then we have to take into account that each waste picker has control of certain resources and an interest in specific resources and events, and social capital is made from particular resources available to him or her. Social capital is defined by its function. It is not a single entity but a variety of different entities, with two elements in common: they all consist of some aspect of social structures, and they facilitate certain actions within the structure. Like other capitals, social capital is productive, making possible the achievement of certain ends that in its absence would not be possible. Unlike other forms of capital, social capital is inherent in the structure of relations between community members. Alternatively, in the second view, we can see the market as consisting of a set of individual retailers, each having an extensive body of social capital from which to draw, through relationships with individuals or families of waste pickers.

To reiterate: on one hand, the state and elite society ignore the existence of the waste pickers; on the other hand, the waste picker community prefers this position in order to avoid the authoritarian approach of the state and to keep their economically and socially profiteering position. Progress against marginalisation is, then, essentially limited.

6 Kinship and neighbourhood

Life without husbands and fathers

Perceptions of kinship and neighbourhood strongly inform my research into the marginalisation of the waste pickers of Calcutta, and I am drawn to Putnam's theories of bridging-bonding and the related areas of social and human capital for context. My ethnography (2011–13) highlights the different ways in which the economic, socio-cultural, ritualistic, consumption and sexual needs of the waste pickers are expressed in their domestic and community lives.

The waste pickers might originate from different districts, states and backgrounds, but when they congregate in the Topsia and Park Circus settlements, they form a fringe community. They share a common interest that is alien to a mainstream society they have neither a wish to join nor to antagonise. This, according to Mr Ali, a key NGO representative, gives them a natural alignment. Together, they shelter on illegal plots close to their work area or dumping grounds, which suits both them and the waste retailers and wholesalers for whom they work. Gradually they form a community, not out of any mainstream sense of kinship, but united in this neighbourhood proximity and their shared, illegal profession. It is overwhelmingly the women who are the constant figures – it is easier for the men to up and leave – as they are responsible for caring for their families. Increasingly, they are doing this alone when their men do either abandon them or spend significant amounts of time in their 'leisure' (generally addiction-related) pursuits. With this being so, my focus is primarily on the role of the women in the settlements: how they live their lives without male figures and the impact this has on them, their children, the neighbourhood and wider society.

Case studies: family life and social life

I will concentrate on the families of two women, Nazma and Husna, with whom I carried out periods of participant observation, and shall refer to other female-headed waste picker families as appropriate. I'll start with some background on the primary families:

Nazma Bewa (who was first introduced in Chapter 3) is a 45-year-old matriarch, literate without formal education, and has power and influence within the community. Her husband has left her and their children (daughters: Seema, 22;

Rina, 20; Phulmoni, 13; and son: Rasul, 9), and Nazma's son-in-law, Sohail Khan, lives with them, as does her granddaughter (Tumpa, 3, Seema's daughter), while her son stays in a hostel at an Islamic religious school (Madrasa), the fees for which are an expensive Rs.1,000 per month. Nazma, who looks pale and ill, is recovering from tuberculosis and only recently started waste picking again. She shivers from the physical exertion and it appears she is forcing herself to work. Her elder two daughters are in good health, but the youngest daughter, Phulmoni, has been tested HIV positive, and community gossip has it that the source of infection is Nazma – a very beautiful woman – who, according to her neighbours, may have had sexual relations with many men. Nazma, herself, says Phulmoni contracted the disease via a blood transfusion in a government hospital where she was being treated for severe diarrhoea.

This family frequently offered me delicious and nutritious food, such as coconut water and nuts, which differed from their regular diet. When I was hesitant to accept, Nazma convinced me that my sharing their food would be their blessing on the path to heaven; they could take no material wealth with them. She pointed out that her granddaughter shares her toys with her neighbourhood friends and Seema cooks rice for her neighbour friend who is suffering from fever (although Nazma scolds her for sharing food. Her insight and experience leads her to think that this will cause future quarrels and misunderstanding). Taking sweets, I participated in their Bakhr-Eid festival, and they seemed very happy that I ate lunch with them.

Nazma's family migrated from Bangladesh a long time ago. Her language is a mixture of Calcutta Bengali and Bangladeshi dialect. Nazma is a complex character, a combination of fighting spirit, religious resignation and an unhappy soul because her husband left her when she was still young. At that time she settled with another woman in Howrah, a neighbouring town on the other bank of the Hooghly. Nazma owns – jointly with her husband – some landed property in Murshidabad, (in the north of West Bengal), of which he took control. When Nazma followed him to her in-laws' house in Murshidabad to ask him why he was depriving her and his children of the land and to seek his blessings, he gave her a paltry sum of money, which she was happy to get; it offered her a little satisfaction in her fight. Back in the settlement, while Nazma was in Murshidabad, her son-in-law, Sohail, stopped working and started to play and gamble every day. I first met him among the card-players in a shabby community room. Sohail is 20–22 years of age and was initially reluctant to speak to me – disturbed when I visited the gambling den, fearing I intended reporting back to his mother-in-law. After several days, he trusted me enough to share his woes about family life, primarily that he feels bullied by Nazma. Her counter-argument is that he takes drugs and alcohol and is, she says, a lazy, gambling man who has already started to neglect his wife, Seema. Nazma has to nag Sohail to go out with her for the collection, she complains: 'My daughters are nice, they work hard, but this son-in-law is a useless fellow. He never wants to work.' Rasul, Nazma's son, also dislikes him. From my point of view, I met Sohail so many times but found no evidence of him being an addict; I felt that he was a shy man.

Nazma calls Seema a gem of a girl, and worries Sohail is a misfit for her. Seema, who seems to be a very understanding woman, tries to defend her husband even though he is neglecting her. Seema has to look after the entire household. She cooks food for the whole family and cleans the room (10 ft by 10 ft, bamboo plastic structure) where all seven members of the family live together. The bed is a well-built double bed, raised from the floor by bricks placed under its four legs. Seema and her husband sleep under the bed while Nazma, her other children and her granddaughter sleep on it. Rina, the second daughter, goes to her work (stitching and tailoring in a shop) early in the morning. Rina, aware she is very beautiful, can be quite demanding, especially of jewellery: metallic ornaments and decorative materials. Phulmoni, the HIV-positive child, sometimes goes to the NGO school but cries constantly when she falls ill. She rarely plays with her niece and quarrels with her about food and toys. The neighbourhood mocks her because of her HIV-positive status, but Nazma has a strong personality and keeps this in check. Rasul, when at home, helps his mother and elder sister with cooking and cleaning. Nazma and Rina have their own mobile phones, one of which went missing when I was visiting. They suspect one of the drug addicts stole it from their house when they were sleeping at night; they do not have a proper lock. They had no difficulty affording a replacement the next day.

The only happy event I observed in their life, apart from the Eid festival, was Rina's engagement, to which Nazma repeatedly invited me. I attended for the whole day, leaving before the evening. In the morning I reached their shelter to find them taking half-showers, except for Rina, who was entitled to a full shower on her special occasion. Rina wore a bright, flashy dress; Seema a decent one and the others changed into their 'best'. They cleaned the room, and prepared some traditional songs to present in the evening. The family does not favour the Bollywood culture, which they consider a Pakistani influence, and evil in their eyes.

Head of the second family, Husna Begum, is from Canning but has settled in Field Area II for her waste picking profession. Her husband abandoned her a long time ago, after which Husna was solely responsible for maintaining her household; she reared the children alone as her husband gave up all contact with the family when he remarried. After living alone for a period, Husna has recently come here to live with her eldest daughter and family (husband and three children) and now she spends her whole day picking up waste from the nearby vat. She regrets that the place (Park Circus Railway Squatters) has nothing to offer: no money, no social life, no cultural life, no love life.

Husna and her daughter's family have no other relatives here, but they do have some roots in their village. This situation is more or less characteristic of the area, and is reflected also in Nazma's situation. It's Catch-22: whenever the waste pickers return to the city after visiting their native villages, their relatives, knowing they earn a reasonable amount in the city, and earn a 'comfortable' living, demand the waste pickers send money 'home'. If they do not transfer this surplus, they will be denied kinship and marriage alliances. These ties remain very significant precisely because of the general lack of blood relatives (beyond the immediate household set up) and automatic kinship bonds within the waste picker settlements. Women have no choice but to – struggle to – look after the family on their own after their husbands have left. Traditionally, they would lose interest in life and it would be rare that they married again but the current younger generation of women are more likely to remarry.

In the Park Circus area my informants revealed that they always try to build up some kind of kinship through their marriages – whether these be within the waste picker community or in the family's respective villages. Husna Begum says that the waste picking families are now marrying boys and girls from families who belong to other professions, such as rickshaw pullers, masons or their assistants, and day labourers. Arjina Bibi (NGO, Tiljala SHED volunteer), is another waste picker from this settlement and her husband sometimes works as a rickshaw puller and occasionally assists the construction workers. Arjina Bibi has a good relationship with her sisters-in-law from both sides; her husband's sisters (Marijan Bibi and Sabjan Bibi) and her brother's wives (Asma Bibi and Arjan Bibi); their husbands are rickshaw pullers, van pullers and waste pickers. These cross-community marriages are happening because young people, these days, are mixing more freely among themselves, which leads to so-called love matches. Such marriages are facilitated by NGO intervention and the waste pickers' own rise in income. However, love matches do not necessarily triumph, and the older generation remains keen on the older traditions adhered to in the village. Returning there with sons and daughters of the right age, they will receive marriage proposals for them that are then negotiated with their rural relatives. If there is any inkling of a city love match, however, action might be taken sooner. I saw first-hand how mothers appear to be most intuitive about their offspring and are generally the first to learn about their daughters' love affairs. While some marriages are arranged in the waste pickers' urban locality, many mothers will take their daughter back to their home village where marriage to an (often) unknown boy is quickly arranged. Initially, the women try to convince their daughters of the benefits to them of marrying their family's choice of man, and the girls do tend to place their trust in their mothers. However, if this fails, they have no compunction about changing tactics and 'terrorising' their daughters instead – though they would call it prudence – and will use subterfuge. It's common for a woman to take her daughter back to the village for two to three months, in the name of relaxation, after a period of intensive waste picking. They will have saved enough money to live quite luxuriously in the village, which is much less expensive than Calcutta, and as a result, there is no shortage of suitors, and in addition, relatives can sometimes use pressure on the mothers to give their daughters into the hands of any suitable groom. In turn, the mothers of boys search for nice domestic kinds of girls for their sons; preference is given to those who are proficient in domestic chores. Once the marriage is decided upon, it is the mother who buys the required van for the groom and gives money to the groom's family as dowry. She also throws the feast for the relatives.

These arranged marriages tend to be set very early; on average the girls get married at 14–15 years old. This is deliberate, to counteract the constant threat of girls being raped or sexually violated; parents worry their daughters will become pregnant or get involved in 'dirty' sexual practices, or that pimps will persuade the girls into prostitution. There is also the simple belief that younger girls get the best husbands. While a general lack of awareness, enhanced by illiteracy, does push parents to arrange early marriages for their daughters, Mr Alamgir, of the NGO, confirms that the parents are often forced to accept them due to the behaviour of the younger males of the community. He says that these boys have no value system and a criminal mentality. They grow up seeing waste, they listen to waste, they earn by waste and all the day they handle waste; meeting young girls inside the frame of waste, they look at love and sex from a very abnormal angle. Although they marry in the name of love, actually they are sexually harassing the girls – and disturbing their parents to get what they want. For example, they threaten households with dangerous materials like hand-made bombs or putting arms inside the shelters during the night, or calling the police on them. Such behaviour confuses and frightens the parents and they feel unable to deny these boys – the husbands they must welcome into their homes. Young girls who get married aged between 15 and 16 years usually live in the same family unit as their mothers. Almost all of them give their earnings to their mothers to run the family, though some keep part of the money for themselves; to purchase cheap cosmetics, sandals, ornaments or their favourite snacks. However, their pattern of expenditure is very different from that of the boys; they do not make habitual purchases. It is one instance of how mothers control their daughters even in a largely undisciplined environment – it is only when daughters fall in love that the mothers are, in some cases, helpless and the girls marry their own choice. Nowadays, mothers are becoming increasingly cowed by their daughters' attitudes and this is where taking the girls to the home villages comes in. Sometimes, as well, the mothers take away their daughters' work so that they cannot marry independently.

There is frequently a question of the legality of marriages, registration and divorce within the waste picker community. For example, Anjura, a 12-year-old girl eloped with a boy and married him. When she gave birth to a baby with severe malnutrition, she simply returned to her mother. In another case, a girl (sister of Sabnam, another waste picker) was married to a boy from Kashmir because her parents were attracted by the idea of their daughter enjoying the fruit gardens and other luxuries there. After the marriage there was no news of her, and her family borrowed money to go to Kashmir, to learn from her in-laws the girl had been sent home and was last seen aboard a train to Calcutta. She was never found and her family was shattered.

These are extreme cases, but sadly for so many of these young married people, there is no happy ever after. Male waste pickers exploit women as a part of daily life. A total of 80 per cent of the male waste pickers are to varying degrees addicted to alcohol, cannabis and hard drugs. They earn around two to three euro per day, which in India is comparable to the income of other poor communities but these men are so reckless and selfish that they only contribute an average of 50 cents to their family for their own food. They cook just the food they need in addition to the rice and vegetables they receive every day from the Christian charity. Moreover, they aggressively demand a share of the family's cooked food. If they need extra money, they extort and steal from their wives and mothers. They believe that they have a right to this without contributing anything towards the children or the family generally. Their addictive behaviours alone incur significant costs, and Hamida, from Topsia, is a woman caught in this cycle of male addiction. Supported by her son, Shohaib, they both claim his father, Munna, has long been an alcoholic. After only a few days of marriage, Munna left his regular work and began to depend on Hamida's jobs: waste picking and working as a cleaner for the NGO. Occasionally he earned money from repairing electrical equipment in the neighbourhood, but even then he never paid for his children's coaching or education fees and rarely gave them change to buy toys and sweets. Women like Hamida are not meek and forgiving about their husbands' behaviours. They are angry and full of angst, citing concrete examples of how reckless and neglectful actions affect their families. For Hamida, conflict extends into her search for fuel; the family must gather bamboo fuel and, as it nears dusk, she is the one left to fight with the next-door neighbour for a few thin fuel logs.

It appears, too, that these traits start young. Hamida complains that all the boys are lazy about their studies. They trick her and, instead of studying, go to the cinema or collect different types of toys from the garbage and play with these – for example, metallic chains and plastic pistols. They do not work regularly; even young boys keep their own money to themselves. They have their lunch and dinner with their families and take their quota of snacks from outside. They are inconsistent in their behaviour; they may or may not give money to their mothers, depending on their mood, and only rarely do they offer them 20–30 rupees (40 cents) a day. They spend a lot on their appearance and fun, including fashionable clothes, entertainment with friends and their favourite foods. At a very early age, 10–12 years, they start to gamble by betting small sums of money on their childhood pastimes like playing marbles, and then they move on to games of cards. Substance addictions also set in at the same time, when they develop a taste for chewable tobacco, quickly using 10–15 packets a day. It's a habit that kills their appetite and destroys their teeth.

Husbands often cannot maintain their relationships with their families, and addiction is frequently cited as the reason. These men leave their wives and marry the other woman. Being Muslim they may take multiple wives and many take two or three, rather than visiting prostitutes. Local NGO members never interfere to tackle this problem: 'We don't represent the government that we are going to tackle each and every problem of these people! We have other work too.' These are the words of Mr Ali. It is an attitude that leaves many women and families very vulnerable to abuse. Noorjahan, aged 20 years, the daughter-in-law of Marijan, tells a chillingly subtle story of the control to which she is subject. She studied to Class 10 and is a very dutiful woman with two children, but is unhappy because she wants to learn sewing and her husband (also 20 years old) has debarred her from the sewing class. He uses violence against her and he repeatedly becomes emotionally involved with other women. If these women hurt or anger him, or his family chastise him, his reaction is to self-harm by cutting his hands and veins. In addition, whenever Noorjahan's husband drinks alcohol, he beats his wife, and, if she intervenes, his mother too.

All in all, my ethnography demonstrates that if early marriage is intended to protect young women, it is failing dismally. Equally, it does little to limit pre-marital romantic and sexual experimentation. During puberty, working in a mixed environment, alongside the strong influence of Bollywood, both girls and boys acquire the concept of 'romantic' feelings and may well start to have sex, married or not, in their early teens. Partly due to the scarcity of other forms of creative entertainment, unprotected sex remains one of their most attractive amusements in life, and despite repeated campaigns by the NGOs, condom usage remains very low. Coming from fragmented families and often deprived of love and affection from their parents, they settle down all too easily with the opposite sex, thinking that their lovers really do love them and will be the ultimate shelter against the hostile world. Husna commented on love marriages in detail, describing how the girls and the boys meet each other while out waste picking, and fall in love – or at least think they do. They elope with each other, returning after a short period, with small children who are suffering from malnutrition. When the honeymoon period passes, the young couple become bitter towards one another. The girls especially suffer; they give birth at a very early age and the men abandon them. As the girls earn their own money, they too could remarry after break-ups; however, they have also accumulated children from (probably) 13–14 years old. So, they settle down with their mothers – after all, their own father is likely to be long gone too.

The waste picker community maintains strong double standards. The husbands lodge severe objections towards wives/partners who maintain platonic friendships with other men, but the husbands can have multiple relationships (in marriage or partnership) at the same time. If a female is caught having an affair or friendship with another male, she faces extreme hostility and probably a severe thrashing from her husband. It is a humiliating situation for the girls and women, restricting even their innocent movements. During my fieldwork and participant observation, four particular stories about the waste pickers' love lives really resonated with me, and Hashura, a volunteer from the community, was certainly one of these innocents. She joined the drama group of the NGO, and was clearly the most intelligent actor present. She soon developed a friendship with another man from the same community and her problems began. Other women informed her husband that Hashura's sole reason for attending the drama group was to see that man; he was furious and refused to allow her to go again. From then on he suspected her all the time. Once, when Hashura went to visit her aunt's house, the neighbours spread a rumour of her spending two days with the man in question. When she returned, she was tortured by her husband and all but locked up inside the house, not even allowed out for garbage collection. She complained about the situation – all caused by gossip and hearsay – to her parents but they were unsympathetic, telling her to settle down peacefully with her husband. Hashura's alleged lover then got married and the whole incident cooled down. Six months later, Hashura and the man revived their friendship and faced the same hostility from both their families. It appears that this kind of secret relationship is both common and not actually secret; the neighbourhood always knows or surmises. Jealousy and non-comprehension over such liberating relationships drive people to make too much of the situation and refuse to accept its innocence.

My second story involves Kohinoor, from Topsia. Her husband left her and their children and they now live with her parents. All of them are waste pickers. Kohinoor has relationships with a number of people through which she earns extra income to support her family. After dusk, she takes them into her room where they drink alcohol, talk and engage in sexual intercourse. Since Kohinoor's main lover is a middle-aged criminal, the local people never uttered a word against her, until one day when neighbours caught them in a compromising situation. The couple were beaten and taken to the police, then released due to lack of proof. Club members and religious leaders who intervened defended their violent actions by saying that it was for the benefit of Kohinoor's own, and local, children who should not be party to such immorality. Kohinoor and her children still live in the same place, and the situation is peaceful now, although the neighbours no longer interact with her. Kohinoor's behaviour is taboo but no one can actually do anything as she has the support of her lover and her parents.

Then there is Rizia, who maintains the most taboo relationship of all: she lives outwardly with her brother-in-law in the waste picker settlement while her husband remains in their home village. Rizia has contracted STDs from one of the two men, meaning both have, in turn, had physical contact with other women. It's a complex situation. Rizia is not like Hashura and Kohinoor; she is open about her arrangements and is harsh and very dominant – if people don't like her situation, tough; it's none of their business. Her two daughters are waste pickers only because she forces them to work as such, and at the same time, she also makes them work as domestic helps. Everyone is wary of Rizia but the most anyone can do is to advise her and her two sexual partners – even though it falls on deaf ears – to have a thorough check-up regarding their sexual health.

Finally, Lakshmi's story falls at the extreme end of the spectrum. Her mother; sister, Selma, and brothers are waste pickers, her husband a taxi driver, and Lakshmi, herself, unemployed. She fell into the habit of bringing home different men, and there was uproar about her relations; her mother even publicly cursed her. A few days after that, in December 2012, Lakshmi was dowsed in kerosene oil and burned alive by her husband. Consequently, her sister Selma's husband grew suspicious of her and threw acid at her eyes, destroying one of them. They stayed together and had four children before the husband abandoned Selma and married another woman from the village. Selma, angry with her husband for betraying her, then married the brother-in-law who had killed her sister, Lakshmi.

Beyond the realms of their waste picking work, family life and perspective tends to be very narrow. Role model Nazma is, in her own way, religious and spiritual; she has sent her son Rasul to the Madrasa school-cum-hostel so that he becomes a decent, educated man. Rasul is a quiet boy and in this almost illiterate world he is an educated child with Urdu and Arabic language skills and mathematical ability. He has a calm relationship with his mother. Nazma's eldest daughter, Seema, is unconsciously liberal and declares that she is fond of all religions, especially of Hindu religious festivals like Durga Puja and Chhot Puja. Nazma is not pleased with this unusual stance, warning Seema it may bring trouble to the house. The sole shared leisure activity and only exposure to culture for this family is watching serials and films – on a television connection and electrical supply that are illegally acquired. In trying to analyse these trashy serials, and discuss them with me, they engage with the fact that there is a kind of depression in the TV stories, which is similar to their own fates. In general, girls are more or less prisoners within their shelter; Seema's sisters cut rubber without taking breaks. I also asked Nazma's neighbour, Hamida, why her daughters never joined in the games outside with their brothers – their family has a rabbit as their shared pet, and this is the girls' only regular entertainment. Hamida said, 'What can I do for them? They are girls. They will have to work. I can understand their sadness. But I am helpless.' She covered up her frustration by saying, 'Anyway we come to this world as beggars and leave as beggars.' Still, I have observed how the girls become melancholic and intuitively aware of their repressive situation even if they cannot verbalise it.

The boys, after returning from their waste picking (or absconding), have a small lunch of drab food (their words) and may go outside to play games including marbles. They play Boss Out or Long Tawl, in which the marbles are aimed at the wall and they roll back to gain positions and drive opponents' marbles out. By investing small amounts of money on the outcome, they find both the game and the gambling exciting. They regularly invited me to watch their games; I did so, watching intently their expertise in handling the marbles. It is debatable whether they are wasting their childhood and intelligence in playing such games repeatedly day after day, or whether this is their escape from their stolen childhood and the hardship of everyday life. So many children, like Shahrukh, a child waste picker from Topsia, never go to any kind of educational institute and such children are increasingly consigned to this subliminal existence. Moreover, growing up with neighbours who are drug addicts and abusive must have an impact, making them both unresponsive and toughened to the harsh realities of their lives. Despite this, the children are not lacking in creativity. For example, when I tried to encourage them to play some other more creative games, they were interested and tried to act and copy the role of a film star (hero). And they have initiative; I watched them level out and prepare the uneven and broken roads with dust using their own hands to make their playgrounds. Rarely do the older children join the younger ones, though. Younger neighbourhood girls imitate rail wagons and recite poems – 'Railway engine making noise like hush-hush-hush'. The smaller boys, refused admission to the marble games, join the girls in imitating different animals like the cow, goats, etc. They play some children's drums and dance to the beats. Another very popular game is targeting birds with their catapults.

For many of the – female – waste pickers, the reading of their religious texts is a frequent and serious pastime. They may not go to schools, but they learn the Urdu and Arabic languages to read their religious texts when they are not working. The community tends to rigidity in its religious beliefs, whether or not this carries over to actual practice. Rituals, however, are a different matter: these, starting with birth and ending with death, are always observed. An infant's head is shaved five days after birth. The moulavi (Islamic priest) whispers the Ajan (the chant of birth which carries the spirit of the morning) in the child's ear. After 40 days the same events are repeated. The infant is washed, dressed in new clothes, and then carried to the mosque for blessing; an occasion to which the parents cannot invite people (a regular practice in mainstream society) due to lack of financial resources. After five years they perform the ritual of Mushalmani and the Zara, when the male children are circumcised. This is supposed to be optional, but the waste pickers follow it as a compulsory ritual. Interestingly, there are two other important rituals, carried out in mainstream Islamic society, that are not performed by the waste pickers. These are Hakika: distribution of goat meat, one for girls and two for boys; and Satka, in which children shave their heads, and their parents weigh the hair and give them an equivalent amount of money.

The ritual of marriage, simplified, still remains the most expansive and expensive for the waste picker community. Mainstream Muslim marriage celebrations continue for an elaborate three days, during which the turmeric ceremony is first, and Mehendi night, when the bride's hands are decorated with henna, takes place the next day. Here, earthen pots with holy water and a bamboo sieving strip are carried by the bride and groom respectively, with the women and the children trailing this procession singing marriage songs. The marriage itself takes place on the third day with lavish food and dancing. Needless to say, things are simpler in the waste picker community, where the wedding occurs within one day, as dictated by work and financial constraints. In the morning, the turmeric is pasted and the impending marriage is announced over the public address system (a loudspeaker). In the evening the Nikah is done, the contractual part of the marriage ceremony, as transcribed by the moulavi (priest). The bride and the groom repeat the marriage chants and have to agree to accept each other. In the waste picker community, the bride's father gives 7,000–8,000 rupees (€9) or a cycle van to the groom to facilitate carrying garbage, and the groom gives 1,500–2,000 rupees (€20). These financial matters, settled in advance when the parents decide how much will be exchanged, are the accounts known as 'den mohor', dependent upon how much the groom earns. During 'taalak' (divorce) the person who initiates the separation has to return all the money to the other party. The Walima, the ceremony traditionally performed in the groom's house, is rarely performed. Simply, the groom arrives at the bride's house two days after the marriage and takes her home with him. Only the bride and groom wear – cheap – new outfits and the major enjoyments are eating biriyani, despite the poor quality rice and meat being quite tasteless, and dancing, following each and every song and step from Bollywood.

I asked Hamida, who used to live with her husband, Munna, in Rajabazar, a predominantly Muslim part of north Calcutta, if there was any love between them before their marriage and she almost rebuked me for suggesting anyone would fall in love with a dumb kind of person like Munna. They had a traditional arranged marriage; the parents from both sides agreed upon the union and it took place. She told me about the marriage, which took place 15 years ago, and was held with as much pomp and grandeur as was possible in their society. On the day, there were high-powered lights in the room, Hamida and Munna's parents were present with a few people as invited guests, and following custom, they painted their bodies with turmeric paste. Two priests officiated and after much haggling, managed to collect 500 rupees from the two households, to lead the couple in reading the Nikah. Relatives provided them with two sets of new dresses, and in the evening a parcel was sent to Munna's shelter containing Hamida's older dresses. Relatives sung traditional songs like 'Allah-Allah kohoti hain', or 'Shaan bolio, ouroshe ghora mangaya, hain mera Allah'. (We chant Allah's name, and, Oh! Lord we have hired the horses for the marriage with the strength that we have you.) Others provided music by playing the drums.

The reality of both the wedding ceremony and subsequent marriage is often a far cry from starry princess-like dreams, but marriage is still exciting – a day of colour in a drab life – as I found out when I spoke to Afrin, Reshma and Tabassum, adolescent waste pickers, also working on cutting rubber straps for the recycling units. They confirmed that the engagement, Nikah, and relocation of the bride to the groom's shelter, all take place on the same day, and poor people hire the club room inside the community area because it is the only well-built structure in the neighbourhood. Sweets are distributed and boys are offered milk in metal cups. On rare occasions, the bride receives a few silver ornaments, and the groom may receive a watch and a silver ring. The women sit inside the club room and sing religious songs or they play Bollywood songs about marriage over the speakers: 'Main ne tumse bichhar ke' (I am feeling lovelorn after separation from my loving partner); 'Mere sajan ko dua karna' (O God, please bless my lover); 'Tumse pyar karke dil laga liya, mera shaath na chhorna' (I have given my heart to you, do not leave me alone after this). The girls tell me they learn the songs and dances from the television and apply heavy make-up to their faces with glittering colours – lipstick and eyeliner – and they wear chains and necklaces in imitation gold, with bangles and bangle-like ornaments for their feet (payel). They wear salwar suits and shampoo their hair. When I asked the trio to perform some of the songs, it was as if they had been transported into another world. They danced, with the utmost perfection, to a very rhythmic song: 'Dinka chika dinka chika', a very popular dance song from Bollywood, copying the sensual body postures and dramatic scenes from Hindi television serials and Bollywood. Their encore was: 'Mera tuta dil hain' (My heart has broken).

The dowry system is rampant among the retailers. They give €160 or bigger amounts as dowries to their sons-in-law, and the wealthiest retailers give very small illegal flats and second-hand scooters to their daughters and their husbands. Yet, even after this, women still face significant harassment from their in-laws and husbands and, typically, first arranged marriages still fail miserably just after children are born.

Death

At the other end of the spectrum is the community's experience of death and funerals. I interviewed waste pickers Anjura Bibi and Aslam Bhai (Park Circus Community Library: 24/12/2012), with precisely this in mind. Statistically, the average age of death is between 55 and 60 years old and the waste pickers mainly die of pneumonia, cirrhosis of the liver (a by-product of their alcohol consumption) and tuberculosis. After death, the body is either taken to the same burial ground used by mainstream society (when Anjura Bibi's husband died, they buried his body in the Park Circus burial ground) or the deceased is transported to their village by hiring a matador, accompanied by relatives and close friends. The family is obligated to inform the nearby mosque and the shops, which sell all the articles required for a funeral: the coffin and the white cloth to cover the body (known as a luban), and the incense sticks lit to purify the air. Two persons (hajjis) come to wash the body thoroughly, using 40 earthen balls and 40 toothpicks, and 40 mugs of water will be poured over while chanting kalmas. The whole process is carried out on a cheap bed, newly bought. The ritual washing is a very expensive affair and costs almost €50, collected by the family (with other sums related to the funeral rites, from neighbours, relatives and retailers, who are traditionally very generous to the grieving family). The body is sprinkled with rose water and cosmetic kohl is applied to the eyelashes. The relatives look at the face of the dead one by one, and afterwards the face is tied with white cloth. After being bathed, the body is wrapped in white cloth and transferred to the strong, wooden bed (tabud) on which it will be carried to the mosque before processing to the burial ground.

Only adult males are permitted at the burial ground. En route, the family distributes dates and bread to the poor people whom they meet on the road so that the recipients will pray for the dead soul. The grave is two feet deep during the rainy season and two feet in the normal season. Once in the grave, the face is turned towards the west. The white cloth is removed from the face of the dead person and rose water is sprinkled on the body; if it is a female her face will be seen only by the core family members. A bamboo structure is set inside the grave and three layers of soil are then poured on top. When these are in place, the priest chants the ritualistic hymn for the dead. After the reading of the hymn the relatives and the family members give the final shape to the grave. A prayer (Namaz) is read by the Hafiz, who knows the Quran by heart. If the waste pickers can afford more, which is rare, the higher-ranking Mufti comes – he can analyse the Quran and understand the deeper meanings and connotations of dreams in a man's life, as well as guiding the ordinary people in reading the Quran. The Hafiz also reads the dua (well-wishing prayer): 'Please, oh God forgive the dead and I pray for his soul. The dead should rest in peace.' At this point, it is believed that two angels, Munkir and Nakir, come to the dead and ask the following questions: What have you done in your lifetime? Who is your Rab/ Allah? If the dead answers in fear, 'You are my Rab/Allah,' then this means they have committed several sins and negative actions in their lifetime. The good soul will answer, 'My Rab/Allah is the Khuda,' and say, 'My last prophet is Hajrat Muhamad Mustafa,' and so Hajarat Muhamad will pray for the dead soul, that their sins should be forgiven and they should be kept secured from the final destruction (Kayamat) and instead reach heaven/paradise (Jannat).

After completing funeral rites the family and neighbours return home and drink sherbet or juice, and the grieving family are supplied with bread and sweets; they do not cook on this sad day. The reading of Quran continues for 40 days, and on the fortieth the Hafiz collects the Punjabis, pyjama, janemaj (table for reading the Quran), mugs and money that were donated to the family and which will pay for his services. The rite that is performed on this day is called the Milad Sharif, and the highest-ranking priest analyses death, and the afterlife, in terms of the Quran. The family feeds the relatives and the friends prepare and distribute the meal of biriyani. If the dead person had a sweet tooth or a craving for meat or any specific food, then the family will distribute those items among the poorest people. The fakirs are also invited to visit the dead person's house, but before agreeing, they ask what the meal will be. If it is simple vegetarian food, they refuse to attend, but if it is biriyani and meat, they come willingly. Sometimes they charge money, sometimes they take away material goods and food. In the past these jobs were voluntary, but nowadays they are professionalised and mercenary; the fakirs belong to agencies and operate from offices and talk on mobile phones.

Interestingly, Aslam Ahmed, NGO driver and resident in a slum near the squatter settlement, admits that these rites are not in the Quran but have been created so that the community integrity of the waste pickers is maintained. 'Placing the soil, the reading of the Quran and the distribution of food among poor people are the basic funeral rituals,' he explains,

> but we have discovered these rites on the tenth day, when we prepare flour pudding and bread and offer them to the fakirs. On the twentieth day we prepare the lentils, meat and bread. Sometimes we prepare lentils and roasted potatoes instead of meat. We share these foods with our relatives but they refuse to take. The relatives have a superstition that this food cannot be digested by them, especially by the children. Then these foods are redistributed among the poor people.

Aslam Ahmed suggests all these rituals associated with funerals are spiritually useless but provide both kinship comfort and a cultural enforcement of unity in the community.

Family ties, kinship and neighbourhood bonding under scanner

If family bonding is precarious, the waste pickers are fundamentally bound by inherent kinship ties, and this is sometimes evidenced in unlikely scenarios. During my time with Nazma's family, a stranger (to me) arrived, trying to sell a brand new, nice nightdress to Nazma's family. Unaware of his circumstances, I was surprised at both the quality of the item he offered so cheaply and that mother and two daughters unanimously insisted on heavy bargaining. Why, I asked, did they haggle so? They smiled at my ignorance and explained the visitor was a known drug addict who would had stolen the dress from the hawkers' (wholesalers) market, so, of course, they were able – and expected – to squeeze him on the price. Everyone was amused by the whole encounter, and I was struck by the liberality of a society that did not exclude an addict of disturbing appearance and regularly allowed him to sell his stolen merchandise in their vicinity. I understood this as the marginalised waste pickers interacting in solidarity and a certain compassion for other, even more marginalised people within their community. It was also a business transaction, from which all parties received a good deal. Only a short while after, the middle daughter, Rina, was peeling a cucumber while sitting outside their shelter in the common passage way, when another passing addict politely asked, in broken English, for some of the cucumber. He was neither driven away nor abused by Nazma, who nodded to Rina to hand over a portion. Again, it confirmed the act of an inclusive society in which the main negativity comes from these drug addicts (many of them are outsiders) practising their habits in the area. I realised this is allowed to happen for two reasons. First, the community are completely helpless against this kind of social issue, and second, their own family members are involved.

Unrelated, but also interesting about Nazma's family, is the unexpected way in which they consider their cat to be a family member – I had thought 'humanising' pets was a somewhat Western phenomenon. The cat's association with the family goes a long time back; she came to them when her mother died. Nazma explains that the cat regularly follows the duo of mother-in-law and son-in-law when they go out to collect their usual recyclable items from the city streets in darkness. Nazma discourages the cat from following, but it is disobedient and follows them till the last. The animal clearly means a lot to all the family, and in its small way, draws them together. For my part, I was also kindly taken in by Nazma, and her family, and via their generous insights, my research developed significantly. I was saddened when I had to stop visiting them regularly, and they invited me to stay with them again the next year.

Waste pickers demonstrate a distinct pattern of consumption, spending their money on their food and clothes, and, during Eid, buying relatively expensive dresses and going on daily outings. As I've outlined, male spending – only occasionally did I come across men whose lives are organised and who take responsibility for their families – usually supports addiction and alcohol consumption, and is often garnered from female family members, despite this being a kind of sin according to Islamic norms. Females, in order to keep the peace and their husbands, hand over money, giving in when the husbands threaten to move on to other women. And men spend a lot on 'other' women. If, as the ethnography shows, the majority of men have multiple partners, usually only one of these women is from inside the waste picker community; the others they keep outside. They spend more on these women than on their children and their first wife. This is quite a different habit from the men in the slums, because slum dwellers earn less and have to spend a lot of money on house rent, the education of children and electricity and so cannot afford to keep multiple partners. In addition, waste pickers do not have the monitoring system, the accountability, of slum dwellers: the landlords, club members and slum political party workers prevent the breaking of marital moral codes.

As breadwinners, the women frequently take on jobs supplementary to their waste picking. They might be the chief earners in a family, but only 2 per cent of the women have bank savings, and others deposit their money with the chit-funds, which are fake and regularly cheat them. The bulk of their income goes back into the family, with personal expenditure limited to cheap dresses, cosmetics and cable television, and some admit to spending 20–30 cents on an addiction, usually to chewable tobacco of different forms (Gutkha, bidi, beetle leaves). They usually cook for the whole house and eat dinner at home, bringing lunch from the Christian Missionary Charity, but some money also goes on buying breakfast and snacks outside the house. On the other hand, for boys, money is about luxuries not necessities. A major expenditure for them is on sim cards for mobile phones and buying different sets of mobile phones. They never spend on sports, games or the gym. Young girls buy cheap fashion, cheap cosmetics, fashionable cheap hair clips, dresses and shoes. Unlike their brothers, very few girls enter into addiction.

Sabjan Bibi is a unique and exemplary woman in her community; the hero of Field Area II. She can negotiate equally with her peers, with retailers and with the outside world. While her husband is a chronic alcoholic, Sabjan not only works as a waste picker but supplements her income by doing extra plastic sorting at Hannan's go-down, working as domestic help and as a construction worker. She is exceptionally hard-working and earns at least €80 per month, spending all her money on the family – including procuring identity cards for them. She has shown prudence by investing in the future: in the Life Insurance Corporation (a government insurance policy company), by purchasing land in a rural area and making deposits into a pension benefit fund (she will invest 70 per cent and the government's contribution will be 30 per cent). At the age of 60, she will reap the fruits of her savings.

I met Sabjan Bibi on 13 February 2013; a special day when the NGOs were celebrating documentation to end violence against girls. She was arguing with the project coordinator, Ms Krishna Chowdhury, about a prize for a healthcare quiz held a few days back. Apparently, Sabjan Bibi's team won and while they received the best prize among the teams, the whole process disappointed her – the event did not reward all the teams. The coordinator and other women tried to convince her that it was like a children's race; not all the runners could receive prizes. But Sabjan's point was that everyone should receive a token – otherwise what becomes of the NGO teaching of equality and non-discrimination? Her logic could not be faulted and her negotiation skills were evident.

My family-based fieldwork has not only brought to light the strength of so many female waste pickers, mothers and neighbours, it has also debunked another great myth: that of life-long monogamy. There is no question that among the waste picker community, the stereotypical institution of marriage is outdated. Men may always have done it, 'secretly', but these days, girls and boys, young men and women, change their partners and even their spouses frequently. Divorced or widowed women will often remarry, too. This, from the ethnography, is factual, but what is particularly interesting is that while the waste pickers instinctively break the traditional rules and regulations, they do not question the institution of marriage intellectually. The women remain more responsible for their families but they rarely attempt to change the lives of their men, afraid that making a stand will result in violence or abandonment. All sense of moral obligation within the waste picker community lies with the female line. The women have extended their network through the NGOs, participating in the meetings for their children's education and family health care. Sometimes they even join the Association of Waste Pickers to extend their waste business. So it is women who perform the act of bridging which may take this community beyond their ghettoised socio-cultural environment.

The women explicitly take on moral responsibility for the family and the role of provider, despite the exploitation they suffer at the hands of their male counterparts in the family. They break stereotypical societal economic/moral norms where it is considered that men should earn more and take economic responsibility for the family. My research examines this crisis/turning point, noting that the males are retreating into the background in terms of both earnings and taking responsibility for their families and children. The mother–daughter units are becoming the centre of a new moral economy, in spite of their degrading treatment from their men. These patterns of behaviour are causing a process of social fragmentation which may make this society collapse beyond repair. However, there is a ray of hope in that, increasingly, daughters are also taking new partners instead of experiencing the tortures their mothers had to endure.

These are examples of a crisis of social solidarity and the usual institutional norms of marriage, families and kinship. The males, especially, are stimulated by distrust, limiting the community's wider engagement, and can be seen as negatively responsible; they appear engaged in their own pleasures towards a gratification that does not contribute towards 'social good' or close ties. They are also inhibiting networking with the outside world, which could support the community through social bridging. The community as a whole is stuck in the locality, which lacks wider networks and trust. As such, family life, kinship and reciprocity are all in jeopardy.

In Chapter 5, I discussed how non-participation and non-cooperation in mainstream schemes indicate that the waste picker community lacks social capital and has an absence of social and economic support structures. The males, especially, are involved in a host of informal economic activities, yet never claim social welfare benefits or take part in self-help schemes. One reason for the low participation of male waste pickers in community exchanges is that peripheral populations often internalise negative images of the area in which they live. Therefore, they lack trust in their co-waste pickers and neighbours. This perception is fuelled by wider media images of their areas as dangerous; it could be argued that they would be more open to involvement in self-help activities if they lived elsewhere. The everyday reality of poor earnings, crumbling shelters and few or no municipal services can create feelings of powerlessness and fatalism in the community, thus discouraging the waste pickers from becoming actively involved in community and other educational projects. Marginalised communities are conditioned by a bleak acceptance of the surrounding deprivation rather than by any attempt to dilute the negative features of their environment. Similar levels of detachment have been detected in areas of poverty as far away, geographically and culturally, as Europe where marginalised communities were found to not openly display their poverty, instead they were often ashamed of it and tended to retreat to the privacy of their shelter rather than engage in any community exchanges with households with similar problems. Regions of high unemployment, poverty and general deprivation have features of distrust and isolation comparable to those seen among the waste picking community.

The isolation of the community gives rise to informal waste picking and informal markets of recycling. This means that social support networks, like NGOs and funding agencies, must act as negotiators; they mediate with the state when the state is unable to provide employment to its citizens. The community accepts its informal set up and an alternative civic system of sanitation, healthcare, saving and education. In the long run the waste picking community takes refuge in (gender) bonding – gambling, playing low-effort games, watching videos, feeding their addictions. These activities build up their alternative social capital, which should be seen as an efficient strategy for evading their depressing condition rather than a solution to individual or community disadvantage.

From different sources, including waste pickers, and NGO staff and management, I gathered (and have described above) that the community broadly relies upon the neighbourhood for some everyday exchanges and help when they face crises like illness, deaths and funerals. Loaning money in an emergency is also a moment of neighbourly recognition. Occasionally money is exchanged among neighbours for mending and knitting clothes, cooking, decorating households for special occasions, and repairing gadgets like their televisions and mobile phones. This exchange of money is far below formal market rates. More often households among this community do not charge other members of the neighbourhood for the provision of goods and services. Many of the community members prefer to build up favours, which can be recalled at a future date. The development of these networks has been enhanced by the geographical immobility of the community and the effect of the stigma of taking up a polluted profession like picking and selling waste. Male waste pickers prefer to do favours only for those whom they feel will be able to reciprocate at some future date. Hence, seemingly reciprocal activities are based on a shrewd calculation of 'one good turn deserves another', which left those unable to repay favours outside these reciprocal networks. Therefore, even within communities exhibiting bonding social capital, processes of inclusion and exclusion are clearly evident. This brings me to Putnam's notion of the transition from bonding to bridging social capital, which he believes is pervaded by optimism – something that stems from his failure to recognise the inherent inequalities within communities exhibiting social capital. To Putnam, such communities are homogenous and his criticism is that they look inward and therefore reinforce parochial tendencies; it is, for him, their relationship with other communities or networks that constitutes the problem. I think differently, and here, I have demonstrated that the community is itself immersed in internal inequalities, so much so that any transition to bridging social capital is likely to produce unequal benefits. In relation to economic linkages, the community demonstrates how bridging social capital benefits individuals rather than the community as a whole.

My ethnography (2011–13) has unearthed no evidence at all to suggest that the waste picker community is linked by a common reliance philosophy where such is interdependent on risk-taking capacity in terms of economy and social capital. Instead, when the NGOs offer the waste pickers options like the building up of an association for waste pickers or common saving schemes, their cooperation is limited. They do not develop movements to promote good health care or education for their community, rather they retreat into the heavily disputed social environment in which they live out their daily lives. The logical conclusion is that their lives are a rollercoaster: full of contradiction, sporadic contributions of help and solidarity from the retailers and sometimes neighbours, and a basic distrust of those around them. The waste pickers do have some exchange points but these cannot be agglomerated in any network. Their common participation in a whole range of social support networks is neither extensive nor intensive. In short, they are not rich in social capital. They negatively nurture inequality and become involved in networking with retailers instead of their peers. Often the motivation to help one another is tainted with self-interest and this is apparent in the process of reciprocity. For instance: if waste picker A does something for waste picker B and trusts B to reciprocate in the future, this establishes an expectation in A and an obligation on the part of B. This obligation can be seen as a credit slip held by A for fulfilment by B. If A holds a large number of credit slips, for a number of persons with whom A has relations, then the analogy to financial capital is direct. These credit slips constitute a large body of credit that A can call in if necessary – unless, of course, the placement of trust has been unwise, and these are bad debts that will not be repaid. There are always a large number of these credit slips outstanding, often on both sides of a relationship. Any informal market can be highlighted as an example. In the waste picker community the credit slips either cancel each other within the community or they are now and then exchanged with the retailers. As the retailers are apparently more self-sufficient and depend on the waste pickers less than the waste pickers depend on them, very few credit slips are in the waste pickers' hands.

This success of this form of social capital depends on two elements: the trustworthiness of the social environment, which means that obligations will be repaid, and the actual extent of obligations held. Social structures differ in both these elements, and actors within the same structure differ in the second. It is an important aid to economic development, but without a high degree of trust among the members of the community the organisation/association could not exist. A person who receives a pay-out of obligation early could abscond and leave the others with a loss. For instance, it's not possible to imagine a rotating credit system operating successfully in urban areas marked by a high degree of social disorganisation, such as defines the waste picking community. Therefore, it is obvious why the waste pickers cannot sustain the association organised by the NGO or are sceptical about joining it.

Alternatively, the club secretary and club members can, by effective use of resources, build up a set of obligations from other local organisations, and such a concentration of obligations constitutes social capital that is useful not only for this local club but increases their potential for action. Involved club members become more powerful than those without extensive credit and debits because they can use the credits to effect more from the waste pickers (and it is well recognised that those in the club are more powerful than those outside it).

It will have become apparent from my research that children are also affected by a lack of socio-human/cultural capital. In Nazma's family, the education and achievement-oriented ambitions of her daughters and granddaughter are neglected, whereas her son has been sent to a (costly) religious educational institute. These females may well have pursued educational or other achievement-oriented activities if they had had some socio-human/cultural capital. Nazma herself is not educated, but her enterprising nature has pushed her to continue her waste picking business – though it has not helped her family in achieving human or social capital. She says she is not callous about her family's socio-human/cultural capital but she is sad and angry that her skills are not recognised and her husband has not given any support since her last child was born. Hamida, with her family, constantly tries to better her children, but is up against children who understand first that their work is profit-oriented and, second, that their daily needs can be fulfilled if they adjust to their living conditions and do without a serious education. Their father is completely negligent and does not concern himself with their education or welfare.

The lack of human/cultural capital could be considered irrelevant if the state provided the waste pickers with an appropriate amount of social capital in their work place or informal education. However, the state has utterly failed. The NGO also never caters to serious education. In Chapter 2, I discussed how the NGO lacks the capability to build up a concrete, focused educational curriculum and language/mathematical programmes. My ethnography suggests that neither social capital (social relations within families and between neighbours or that provided by the mainstream) nor human/culture capital are able to fulfil the education of the community. Similarly, the research periodically assesses the strength of relations between family members, the neighbourhood, the retailers and mainstream society/state, and by measuring the strength of relations and the waste pickers' investment in socio-cultural capitals such as education and healthcare, it is possible to explore different levels of ideological marginalisation. Socio-cultural capital gives the children and adults of the community access to mainstream human capital (i.e. education), yet it is contingent on the attention given by both the parents to the children and that given by the state/mainstream society to the waste picker community as a whole. The physical absence of the parents or the state/mainstream may be described as a structural deficiency in terms of the community socio-cultural capital (Coleman 1988). The lack of strong relations within families is in part an effect of the male children's embeddedness in a youth community, an echo of their fathers' embeddedness in relationships with other adults in the neighbourhood. The female children suffer most as they cannot go out after work and they receive little encouragement from their parents. To date, the waste picker community's backlog in social capital is so extensive it will not be able to acquire the required cultural or human capital in the near future. This results in an ever-increasing number of school dropouts among the community children, something that cannot, however concerted an effort, be controlled by the NGO. Generally, any education of the children is directly related to the mother's expectations and effort (the fathers being so often absent or apathetic), which is why Nazma stretches herself to afford the boarding school fees that will secure her son's future.

Despite the criticisms outlined in this research, one of the advantages of the concept of social capital is how it has brought older values, altruism, obligations, trust, reciprocity, networks and community, once more to the forefront of anthropological inquiry. A more rigorous interrogation of the key longstanding concepts that social capital uses in its formulation would reveal much more complicated, multi-layered processes of inclusion and exclusion than Putnam's notion of bonding and bridging social capital permits. Making the transition from bonding to bridging social capital may not necessarily lead to the positive outcomes he envisages, but rather reinforce existing social, economic and cultural inequality. When the waste pickers lived in their rural villages it could rightfully have been said that they had stronger social capital, including bonding and bridging with their kin and neighbourhood. But over the last decade the urban waste picker community has faced severe shrinking of its social capital. This trend may well be due to the increased number of women in the workplace and increased mobility of families, which results in the 'obliteration of traditions' including the resultant lack of independent civic engagement and a widespread tendency toward the passive reliance on the waste pickers' inward-looking attitudes (Putnam 1995). There is certainly a gender divide in the types of organisations joined (though uptake is always poor across the board). Women gravitate to school service groups (mostly parent-teachers meetings), sports groups for the children, and associational meetings. For men, clubs and fraternal groups are relatively popular, but parent-teacher meetings or associational meetings are meaningless. Since the former is a significant form of modern civic engagement, and thus social capital, it is sad they remain unaware, or uncaring, about the potential benefits for their children's future. Where the female waste pickers do show efficiency is in provoking the NGO policies and bringing them inside the vortex of competition with comparative organisations to generate more benefits in terms of food, books and health care. This is a 'whimsical, yet discomfiting bit of evidence of social disengagement' (Putnam 1995). All in all, it is evident that individual waste pickers are becoming prosperous in terms of money but their organised activities are reducing day by day, and their spending habits are often imprudent.

Without doubt, the social capital of the waste picker community is much less than the ideal. The decline of traditional social capital has given rise to electronic entertainment among both men and women in the community, dismantling any other alternative socio-cultural resolutions. The NGO has failed to foster and nurture community solidarity, and especially an ethos of marital support. This has encouraged the males to spend on social interaction and ignore civic conversation, and has restricted the women to engage less in the civic trust and educational and association work for their business. There is a huge dichotomy between man and woman, husband and wife, in the waste picker community, and the women are carrying the practical, moral and kinship roles and responsibilities – and doing a good job of it. Many families survive day in, day out without father figures or good role models, but whether this is good for the waste picker community, now and in the future, is in serious doubt.

7 Conclusion

The waste pickers of Calcutta are a marginalised community; marginalised in terms of any and all definitions I have outlined. Why they are marginalised is apparent on a number of levels, evident in my own research and the theoretical framework that surrounds it. The waste pickers' tale takes it as axiomatic that they are economically destitute and even more that they are dispirited (Wacquant 2010a: 2). The first palpable feature of their daily life that stands out is their material and socio-cultural decay. This is closely followed by a sense of the extreme alienation of the adults of the community, from the state and mainstream society and their focused participation in their non-formal waste business. In short, the Calcutta mainstream society and state have left the waste picker community in a 'state of infrastructural and institutional abandonment' (Wacquant 2010a).

This is, though, not a regional or Indian issue, but a global one. A direct counterpart lies in a similarly ghettoised community of black people in the US city of Chicago, wherein urban desolation is translated into 'collective demoralisation, registered in feelings of dejection, dread and anger, alcoholism and drug abuse, depression and assorted mental afflictions' (Wacquant 2010a: 2). Wherever in the world they are, the continuous marginalisation and stigmatisation of 'second class' community people mean that behaviour towards them can be biased and discriminatory; namely the actions of public authorities, other citizens, commercial operators and state officials. Mainstream society and the state fear that these marginalised people have the potential to harm their properties and resources. With respect to the waste pickers, those from the mainstream who donate recyclable materials never transact with the community people directly because they are suspicious of the community's 'low work ethic and moral standards' (Wacquant 2007a). This discriminatory attitude of the 'opposition' damages the waste pickers' opportunities for social networking and their cultural expectations. They live in despair and frustration and adhere to non-participation in any 'outside' activities and programmes, including those arranged by NGOs as well as by the state. Instead, the adult and adolescent males of the community take up illegitimate gambling, addiction and other negative urban activities (including visiting sex workers even when they have their own families). They change partners frequently, which deeply disrupts families, and they become irresponsible social representatives who are apathetic when it comes to their children's education, health and hygiene. Female waste pickers occasionally participate in external projects and take an interest in their children's education; either way, the children follow their parents' model. They are reluctant to participate in education and invest their spare time in unconventional games, investing small sums of money to have the feeling of gambling. The girls work and play indoor games, dance to Bollywood songs and occasionally enjoy the company of some pet animals.

My ethnography has taken stock of the ideological marginalisation of the waste picking community, and its negotiations with different stakeholders, including NGOs, retailers, the state, people from mainstream housing complexes and corporate firms. The community's marginalisation is attached to the 'brute facts of its physical dilapidation' (Wacquant 2008: 176) as described in the detailed evidence collected from my 2011–13 fieldwork. Their marginalisation is manifested by the community's non-participation in, and abstention from, civic society. The community comes to understand 'the blatant inferiority' (Wacquant 2008: 176) of their position in terms of accessing 'institutions, be they public schools, social welfare schemes, municipal services, neighbourhood associations that survive inside their perimeter' (Wacquant 2008:176). In addition, they always find confirmation of their inferiority in the glaring attitudes of the powerful 'outriders': the banks, NGOs, mainstream/elites, the police and the state. The inevitable process of exclusion from these regular institutions and the economy of the mainstream society influences this marginal community to become 'demoralised' (Wacquant 2008: 177) and distrust the mainstream organisations and institutions.

The waste pickers lack any collective movement for their rights, instead adopting an 'individualistic ideology of achievement' and choosing a path of negotiation with the stakeholders for their survival (Wacquant 2008: 180). Their perennial non-participation in the NGO-arranged education, healthcare system, savings schemes, self-help groups and other training programmes reflect the divided feeling of their community – they refuse to recognise the collective nature of their problem. In consequence they plan strategies of both distancing themselves from mainstream society/the state and NGOs and negotiation with the stakeholders for their freedom from economic marginalisation. These negotiations produce a patron–client relationship in the place of state welfare, indicating the failure of the latter. From my research perspective, the waste picking community as a whole is in crisis, yet in a curious paradox, it stands that the NGOs have largely influenced this outlook; according to the waste pickers themselves, this is not the whole truth. Consider Nazma, the matriarch of the first family with whom I did my initial phase of fieldwork: she was an expert in negotiating with the retailers, and with her neighbourhood as well. In fact, both key women from my two primary families proved the NGO and state's negative notions wrong by their perseverance and discipline in their work. Perhaps they are exceptions to the rule, but I am in no doubt that there are other marginalised women (and men) out there who are quietly holding their families, their lives and their communities together. Surely, they are, in some little way, making their marginalised lives slightly less marginalised.

Nevertheless, powerless individuals, however talented, are limited in what they can achieve without support – especially when the allegedly supportive agencies are themselves lacking. Blatant evidence demonstrates that after 16 years of project work with the waste pickers, the incumbent NGO has failed in many respects to uplift this community, instead it has assisted in placing it in its difficult position. In order to save its own jobs and the project, the NGO has consistently blamed the waste pickers for their shortcomings and complains that the community is uncooperative. The NGOs see the waste pickers refusing to engage in any training/project-oriented work like education, cultural activities and savings schemes and dismissing work through the Association of Waste Pickers, and they conclude that the community is uncooperative and pessimistic in nature and therefore their crisis will never end. This view may be affected by the fact that if this crisis is resolved the NGO will lose this huge project and their jobs. Whether my field colleagues are part of this flip side of the project is a moot point.

The waste pickers are bound to come under state power through 'disembodied abstract contracts' in concrete terms of interactions (Bourdieu 1989). This book has demonstrated the complex, unbalanced relationship between the powerful and the marginalised, and how power mediates and changes the waste pickers' lives. They may position themselves in a zone of autonomy, but in these crucial times the survival strategies of the waste pickers ultimately and inevitably fail. In attempts to maintain this autonomy they develop cultural resilience for themselves, never participate in mainstream projects and avoid state welfare. Power is more dispersed, and it becomes a dilemma for the powerful as to whether they can exploit the powerless (in the eyes of the state) appropriately. For example, the mainstream, elites and state as a body, were not inclined to help the waste pickers even after their 400–500 shelters were gutted by fire on 5 April 2014. Sadly, this is probably only what the community expected; since their childhood the waste pickers have felt the conditions of dispossession. They know – in real terms now – that they will never receive relief or aid from the state even in times of necessity and emergency. The state either did not understand, or did not care about, the urgency of their desperate situation after the fire. The community's pragmatic response was to submerge itself into the necessary struggle of obtaining materials to begin the hard work of rebuilding their shelters. As such, they detached themselves from abstract matters and maintained their autonomy in terms of public/state space and resources – this is their natural reaction to crisis.

Consciously or otherwise, the waste pickers always abstain from the wider structure of mainstream social space, creating their own sub-field. Thus, they try to ignore the inbuilt superiority of the state and sublimate their own crisis of inferiority. They use the hidden symbolic power of their own habitus constituted of possession/dispossession, their negligent parents and neighbours, their own non-formal education and feelings of frustration and marginalisation in any formal setting. They construct their own discipline in their non-formal habitus, absorbing punishment for their rejection of anything formal. This non-formal business of recycling waste run by the retailers and pickers can be seen as an alternative economy running competitively alongside the mainstream market economy. Although they are excluded from the mainstream economic markets, they have gained their own position. This informal market belongs to the informal economic field, as it has many independent and unique operations behind the regulations of the state authority. Waste pickers working on the street know intuitively the rules of the games and the boundaries of practices. The authorities have endured their presence as their businesses are still prevented from using state and mainstream resources. The informal economic field has continued to distinguish itself from the authorised one. In this sense, the informal markets are the safety valve of the state; they help to settle the consumption needs of the urban marginalised community in a private sphere. The unplanned informal economic field has actually connected not only within a local community network, but also with a petty trading network of recycling units and markets. Undoubtedly, the pessimistic outlook within the waste picker community contributes towards their marginalisation as part of the vicious cycle of ideological marginalisation and economic marginalisation. In Chapters 2, 3 and 4 I have laid out how, at present, their lack of social and cultural capital is embodied in their distrust and absence of obligation and reciprocity in regard to all stakeholders: field colleagues, neighbours, NGOs, the elite/mainstream and the state. This absence of social and cultural capital is dominating both their ideological and economic marginalisation.

There is tremendous scope for studying the negotiation skills of waste pickers/marginalised people in terms of their business with the waste retailers. Such skills help them to go about their business despite their lack of social capital/networking skills and human capital, and mean that they can ignore inequality and move tacitly and tactfully to survive. Nowadays, to improve its earnings (in the opinion of the NGO) the community joins the NGO in coordinating with corporate sectors and housing complexes to gain huge donations of recyclables. My research suggests it is necessary to nurture the negotiating skills of a marginalised community in order to develop its social capital and thus begin to eradicate its ideological marginalisation. However, the research equally indicates that the community appears to prefer its seclusion in order to safeguard autonomy as regards its illegal and informal businesses. Herein lies a quandary. The waste pickers do make an effort to maintain a strong rapport with the local, influential waste retailers, who provide them with business and loans, as well as club members, who act as brokers between the community and the outside world. However, the waste pickers are also quite aware that these retailers and club members never consider them as equals. The retailers and the club members have their own businesses based on what the waste pickers supply, but they never share their profits with them. The retailers and club members are from similar localities, but they can offer loans and political connections whenever the waste pickers are in difficult situations. The retailers feed the waste pickers and offer them clothes during festivals and rituals, but they never accept such feasts or gifts from the waste pickers. Such beneficent acts from the retailers ensure that waste pickers are retained and local business runs smoothly and productively but they never enter into any social communication with the waste pickers.

Spatial marginalisation arises when the community is denied the use of public spaces: proper markets, shopping malls, parks, and educational and healthcare institutions provided by the state and other dominant stakeholders. However, my research reveals how this unique community breaks these rules of marginalisation by building their own mud roads inside the core of the city and by making their own informal markets/spaces for buying and selling their recycled products made from plastic, glass and rubber, and expensive metal products. They create their own exotic modes of transport (i.e. motorised tricycles vans) for carrying their waste to the selling points. Thus, the waste picker community creates its own stateless/illegal spaces to run members' lives effectively despite police/state intervention. They innovate and struggle to maintain their freedom and autonomy, and they quite intelligently ignore their subjugation and subordination to the point where, in its urban context, the marginalised community manages to avoid displaying submissive behaviour. The waste pickers are confident in their capacity, despite their skills being utilised in a completely illegal/non-formal and 'polluted' profession. Their philosophy of life is one of non-participation in mainstream life and schemes, and as such they can negotiate their own terms with the NGOs. They demonstrate strength and a kind of pride mixed with stoicism, pessimism, angst and dreamlessness as they face 'segregation and non-reciprocal relations' (Pankhurst 2003: 6) in their lives.

It is at this juncture that my current field work halts; it cannot conclude whether this lack of socio-cultural and human capital or stoic-dreamlessness needs to be changed. That said, there are fundamental human rights that exist regardless of attitude or action: for instance, it would be cruel to demur over the obvious need for proper sanitation, education and healthcare within the waste picking community. Urban planners should keep in mind the process of sustainability for these marginalised communities. Constitutions can encompass such non-citizens as their new citizens while protecting their autonomy and freedom. Here, it is my place to give the waste pickers – these non-citizens, insurgent peoples, marginalised communities (call them what you will) – a voice and stress that they are entitled to all possible options, resources and choices in their lives to build up what Bourdieu, Coleman and Putnam call their socio-cultural capitals. If, on receipt of such options, the community members maintain their distance from the state, well, this choice should still be respected by the state and mainstream society. NGOs, ineffective as they have been, should not take all the blame. They deserve more power in a second chance to demonstrate that they can stand by the marginalised communities more effectively; so far, the state has kept very little room for welfare schemes through the redistribution of wealth. In practical terms, the eviction of community people from their shelters must be stopped – the first step towards giving this community security and insurance.

The fringe areas of Park Circus railway line and the polluted Topsia canal-side squatter settlements in Calcutta, where the waste pickers reside, may be aptly called 'shatter zones or zones of refuge' (Scott 2009). However, they contain every aspect of these people's lives: their work, social organisations, ideologies and even their local cultures, including their cheap film-based culture. This explains their 'strategic positioning' (Scott 2009: x) designed to keep the state at arm's length. Their residence in rugged terrain, their mother–daughter kinship structure and illegal, 'polluted' profession speak not only of their avoidance of incorporation into the state but also of their desire to prevent 'states from springing up among them' (Scott 2009: x). My argument stresses that the contemporary history of 'state making' neglects the conscious effort of the waste pickers to be stateless, sequestered away from taxes and state rules and regulations. A fundamental dimension of my research is highlighting the need to deconstruct discourses that describe these people as 'raw', 'polluted' and morally bankrupt. My counter-argument is to ask why the waste pickers choose their status as non-citizens and non-users of state welfare, and seeks to explain why they refuse mainstream benefits like education, saving schemes and health care. I describe how their location, subsistence and alienated social structures are adopted to evade the state, which means that in the waste pickers' world 'taxes and sovereignty end' (Scott 2009: xi).

Mainstream society members, enjoying the status of state subjects, find it disturbing when they observe that the waste pickers can keep the state at an arm's length distance and maintain their 'self-governing' status by abstention and non-participation. The waste pickers have already refused proper shelters in remote areas away from their work place and have chosen to live in their squatter settlements beside railway tracks and polluted canals. The waste pickers have also ignored the threat by the State Conservancy Section's chief that they should move away to their native villages on their own or be forced to leave. This unique community defies stigmatisation as it draws strength from its firm location at the margins, 'their flexible social structures, their ritualistic heterodoxy, their egalitarianism and even their non-literate cultural heterodoxy' (Scott 2009: 9). The community people's strength comes from their tacit tactics, which are designed to 'evade both state capture and state formation' (Scott 2009: 9). Their profound understanding of the powerful state is that it may seem to be attractive but that at the same time it can be engulfing and 'threaten' their lives.

Marginalised people like the waste pickers of Calcutta are rarely drawn towards a 'fiscally legible economy of wage labour' or the static agro-economics in their native villages. They instinctively presume that their unique business of the collection and sale of recyclable waste gives them all the benefits of trade 'without drudgery and subordination' (Scott 2009: 10) as faced by the elite/mainstream society under the state. NGOs and other charity organisations have attempted to bring them under 'routine administration' and homogenous linguistic, cultural and ritualistic alignment by implementing educational and other projects of association for waste pickers. These programmes have failed in the majority of the cases as the males abstained or participated only in a very casual way. This is despite the fact that the women have more often compensated for this non-participation by joining in different programmes and even encouraging their children to a certain extent. Thus the community, by its location, social structures, subsistence pattern and ritualistic shortcuts, has more or less kept its distance from the state. In the long run it has failed to contribute to the processes of state making and state expansion. Hence the dominant society and state have the scope to blame the waste pickers for their position inside their 'shatter zone and region of refuge'. The state can withdraw from its own responsibility for providing them with state welfare and pull out all the resources from these non-citizens. The cultural positioning of the waste pickers along with their geographical remoteness is an evident tool to measure their degree of 'state evasion' (Scott 2009: 330).

Random migration and the illegitimate transportation of young boys for this profession originally give rise to waste picking and from this, a full squatter community has slowly emerged. Theirs is a non-structured, haphazard profession that has created and now maintains this 'shatter zone' within which there is a constant reformulation and subversion of socio-cultural and human capital. This is a community that internally selects when and how to perform bonding and bridging of social capital. At first its lack of economic capital in successive generations resulted in a deficit of both, something exacerbated by poor networking, mistrust and lack of obligation and reciprocal exchanges. The fall has not been softened by state intervention, and at present, their depreciation of social capital and ideological marginalisation is hampering any economic advancement of the waste picker community. Its ideological marginalisation is expressed in an unquestionable truth voiced by the state/elite and mainstream society – that it is engaged in polluting work. Such an untouchable label perpetuates a vicious circle: the state feels justified in conferring upon the waste pickers a low status and the waste pickers have no collateral to increase their position. By outside society, for example NGO staff and management, they are stereotyped as quick to anger, alcoholic and extravagant; even the NGO secretary, who evinced compassion towards the community, reported how they lack self-esteem and respect. The State Conservancy Section representatives and other mainstream departments unequivocally address the waste pickers in negative terms: anti-social, untrustworthy, unreliable, lazy, liars, cowards and immoral. Their advice is that these 'eyesores to the dominant urban society' disband and return to their native villages.

Simply, there is overwhelming evidence that the waste picker community has limited scope when it comes to opting for an alternate economy and socio-cultural capitals – something that requires recognition from the state and other dominant society members as well as from its own community. Until there is an improved attitude and approach towards waste collection, segregation and selling of the recyclables – and to the people who engage in such activity – there can be no viable development strategy. At the beginning of this book, I referred to Octavio Paz and his concept of 'space'. I stated my intention to explore the way in which the waste picker community creates its own space where its members fit best, but which is misunderstood and distorted by wider society. Through the chapters of this book, I have attempted to do so, and in so doing I confirmed and discussed the chasm that separates the two groups. If I desire one key outcome of my ethnography it is to encourage dialogue between the waste pickers of Calcutta and the state/mainstream society. This alone can be the catalyst for change.

Bibliography

Amborn, H. (1990). *Differenzierung und Integration. Vergleichende Untersuchungen zu Spezialisten und Handwerkern in Sudauthiopischen Agrargesellschaften.* Munich: Trickster.

Appadurai, A. (1986). Theory in Anthropology: Centre and Periphery. *Comparative Studies in Society and History*, Vol. 28, No. 2, pp. 356–61.

Appadurai, A. (1988). Putting Hierarchy in its Place. *Cultural Anthropology Today*, Vol. 3, No. 1, Place and Voice in Anthropological Theory, pp. 36–49.

Appadurai, A. (1996a). *Modernity at Large: Cultural Dimensions of Globalization.* Minneapolis, MN: University of Minnesota Press.

Appadurai, A. (1996b). Sovereignty without Territoriality: Notes for a Postnational Geography. In: Yaegar, P. (Ed.), *The Geography of Identity.* Ann Arbor, MI: University of Michigan Press, pp. 40–58.

Appadurai, A. (2000). Spectral Housing and Urban Cleansing: Notes on Millennial Mumbai. *Public Culture*, Vol. 12, No. 3, pp. 627–51.

Appadurai, A. (2002). Deep Democracy: Urban Governmentality and the Horizon of Politics. *Public Culture*, Vol. 14, No. 1, pp. 21–47.

Appadurai, A. (2006a). *Fear of Small Numbers: An Essay on the Geography of Anger.* Durham NC: Duke University Press.

Appadurai, A. (2006b). The Thing Itself. *Public Culture*, Vol. 18, No. 1, pp. 15–23.

Appadurai, A. (2010). How Histories Make Geographies: Circulation and Context in a Global Perspective. *Transcultural Studies*, Vol. 1, pp. 1–4.

Appadurai, A. and Holston, J. (1999). Introduction: Cities and Citizenship. In: Holston, J. (Ed.), *Cities and Citizenship.* Durham, NC: Duke University Press, pp. 1–17.

Arnold, J.E. (1993). Labor and the Rise of Complex Hunter-gatherers. *Journal of Anthropological Archaeology*, Vol. 12, pp. 75–119.

Arnold, J.E. (1995a). Social Inequality, Marginalization, and Economic Process. In: Price, T. and Feiman, G. (Eds.), *Foundations of Social Inequality.* New York: Plenum Press, pp. 87–103.

Arnold, J.E. (1995b). Transportation Innovation and Social Complexity among Maritime Hunter-gatherer Societies. *American Anthropologist*, Vol. 97, No. 4, pp. 733–47.

Auyero, J. (2011). Researching the Urban Margins: What Can the United States Learn from Latin America and Vice and Versa? *City and Community*, Vol. 10, No. 4, pp. 431–6.

Bauman, R. and Briggs, C.L. (2003). *Voices of Modernity: Language, Ideologies and Politics of Inequality.* Cambridge, UK: Cambridge University Press.

Bhattacharya, M. and Sen, N. (1997). *A Socio-economic Study on the Waste-picker Children of Calcutta.* One World Association.

Binford, L.R. (1983). *In Pursuit of The Past*. New York: Thames and Hudson.

Blok, A. (1988). Book Review of 'The Anthropology of Violence' by David Riches. *Man*, Vol. 23, No. 4, pp. 785–6.

Bourdieu, P. (1983). The Field of Cultural Production, or: The Economic World Reversed. *Poetics*, Vol. 12, No. 4–5, pp. 311–56.

Bourdieu, P. (1984). *Distinction: A Social Critique of the Judgement of Taste*. Cambridge, MA: Harvard University Press.

Bourdieu, P. (1986). The Forms of Capital. In: Richardson, J. (Ed.), *Handbook of Theory and Research for the Sociology of Education*. New York: Greenwood, pp. 241–58.

Bourdieu, P. (1989). Space and Symbolic Power. *Sociological Theory*, Vol. 7, No. 1, pp. 14–25.

Bourdieu, P. (1990). *Reproduction in Education, Society and Culture*. London: Sage Publications.

Bourdieu, P. (1991). *Language and Symbolic Power*. Cambridge, UK: Polity Press.

Bourdieu, P. (2000). *Acts of Resistance: Against the New Myths of our Time*. Trans. Nice, R., Cambridge UK: Polity Press.

Bourdieu, P. and Wacquant, L. (1992). *An Invitation to Reflexive Sociology*. Chicago, IL: The University of Chicago Press.

Braukämper, U. (1984). Ökologische Grenzlinien und kulturelle Wandlungsprozesse zwischen Kamel- und Rindernomadismus im Ostsudan. *Paideuma*, Vol. 30, pp. 81–102.

Brumfiel, E.M. (1992). Breaking and Entering the Ecosystem – Gender, Class and Faction Steal the Show. *American Anthropologist*, Vol. 94, pp. 551–67.

Cerulli, E. (1922). Folk Literature of the Galla of Southern Abyssinia. *Harvard African Studies*, Vol. 3, pp. 200–14.

Cerulli, E. (1930). *Etiopia Occidentale*. Rome: Sindacato Italiano Arti Grafiche.

Coleman, J. (1988). Social Capital in the Creation of Human Capital. Sociological and Economic Approaches to the Anlysis os Social Structure. *American Journal Sociology*, Vol. 94, pp. S95–S120.

Elias, N. (1978). *The Civilising Process: The History of Manners*. Oxford, UK: Blackwell.

Furedy, C. (1984). Survival Strategies of the Urban Poor-Scavenging and Recuperation in Calcutta. *Geojournal*, Vol. 8. No. 2, pp. 129–36.

Furedy, C. (1990). Women and Solid Waste Management in Poor Communities: Resource Scarcity, Women, and Solid Waste Management. Paper presented at the *16th WEDC Conference. Infrastructure for Low-Income Communities*, Hyderabad, India.

Furedy, C. and Ghosh, D. (1984). The Garbage Farms and Sewage-Fed Fisheries of Calcutta: Conservation and Recycling. *Resource Conserving Traditions and Waste Disposal*, Vol. 7, No. 2–4, pp. 159–65.

Furedy, C. and Alamgir, M. (1992). *Street Pickers in Calcutta Slums*. Mimeo.

Giddens, A. and Stanworth, P. (1974). *Elites and Power in British Society*. Cambridge, UK: Cambridge University Press.

Gledhill, J. (2000). *Power and its Disguises: Anthropological Perspectives on Politics*. London: Pluto Press.

Gosden, C. (1989). Debt, Production and Prehistory. *Journal of Anthropological Archaeology*, Vol. 8, pp. 355–87.

Guha, R. (1983). The Prose of Counter Insurgency. In: Guha, R. (Ed.), *Subaltern Studies II*. New Delhi: Oxford University Press, pp. 1–42.

Haberland, E. (1962). Zum Problem der Jäger und besondere Kasten in Nordost- und Ost-Africa. *Paideuma*, Vol. 7, pp. 136–55.

Haberland, E. (1979). Special Castes in Ethiopia. In: Hess R. (Ed.), *Proceedings of the Fifth International Conference on Ethiopian Studies*. Chicago, IL: University of Chicago Press.

Hallpike, C.R. (1968). The Status of Craftsmen among the Konso of South-west Ethiopia. *Africa: Journal of the International African Institute*, Vol. 38, pp. 258–69.

Hart, K. (2002). World Society as an Old Regime. In: Shore, C. and Nugent, L. (Eds.), *Elite Cultures: Anthropological Perspectives*. London and New York: Routledge.

Hayami, Y., Dikshit, A.K. and Mishra, S.N. (2006). Waste Pickers and Collectors in Delhi: Poverty and Environment in an Urban Informal Sector. *Journal of Development Studies*, Vol. 42, No. 1, pp. 41–69.

Hayden, B. (1995). Pathways to Power: Principles for Creating Socioeconomic Inequalities. In: Price, T. and Feiman, G. (Eds.), *Fundamental Issues in Archaeology: Foundations of Social Inequality*. New York: Plenum Press, pp. 87–103.

Holston, J. (1989). *The Modernist City: An Anthropological Critique of Brasilia*. Chicago, IL: University of Chicago Press.

Holston, J. (1995). Insurgent Urbanism: Interactive Architecture and a Dialogue with Craig Hodgetts. In: Marcus, G.E. (Ed.), *Techno Scientific Imaginaries*. Chicago, IL: University of Chicago Press, pp. 461–505.

Holston, J. (1998). Spaces of Insurgent Citizenship. In: Sandercoch, L. (Ed.), *Making the Invisible the Visible: A Multicultural Planning History*. London: University of California Press, pp. 37–57.

Holston, J. (2008). *Insurgent Citizenship: Disjunction of Democracy and Modernity in Brazil*. Princeton: Princeton University Press.

Holston, J. (2009). Insurgent Citizenship in an Era of Global Urban Peripheries. *Cities and Society*, Vol. 21, No. 2, pp. 245–67.

Holston, J. and Appadurai, A. (1996). Cities and Citizenship. *Public Culture*, Vol. 8, No. 2, pp. 187–204.

Huntingford, G.W.B. (1931). Free Hunters, Serf-tribes, and Submerged Classes in East Africa. *Man* (O.S.), Vol. 31, pp. 262–6.

Katz, E. and Lazarfeld, P.F. (1955). *Personal Influence: The Part Played by People in the Flow of Mass Communications*. New York: Free Press.

Kelly, R.L. (1991). Sedentism, Sociopolitical Inequality, and Resource Fluctuations. In: Gregg, S.A. (Ed.), *Between Bands and States*, Southern Illinois University Center for Archaeological Investigations, Occasional Paper No. 9. Carbondale: Southern Illinois University Press, pp. 135–58.

Knudsen, B., Florida, R. and Rousseau, D. (2010). *Bridging and Bonding: A Multidimensional Approach to Regional Social Capital*. The Martin Prosperity Institute, University of Toronto. Mimeo. Available at www.creativeclass.com

Lefebvre, H. (1974 [1991]). *The Production of Space*. [Trans. Smith, D.N.]. Oxford, UK: Blackwell.

Leonard, M. (2004). Bonding and Bridging Social Capital: Reflections from Belfast. *Sociology*, Vol. 38, No. 5, pp. 927–44.

Levine, D. (1974). *Greater Ethiopia*. Chicago, IL: University of Chicago Press.

Marcus, G. (1983). 'Elite' as a Concept, Theory and Research Tradition. In: Marcus, G. (Ed.), *Elites: Ethnographic Issues*. Albuquerque, NM: University of New Mexico Press, pp. 7–27.

Meillassoux, C. (1981). *Maidens, Meal and Money*. Cambridge, UK: Cambridge University Press.

Mitrović, L. (2005). Bourdieu's Criticism of the Neoliberal Philosophy of Development, the Myth of 'Mondialization' and the New Europe. *Facta Universitatis Series: Philosophy, Sociology, Psychology and History*, Vol. 4, No. 1, pp. 37–49.

Narayan, D. and Cassidy, M.F. (2001). A Dimensional Approach to Measuring Social Capital: Development and Validation of a Social Capital Inventory. *Current Sociology*, Vol. 49, No. 2, pp. 59–102.

Pankhurst, A. (1999). Caste in Africa: The Evidence from South-Western Ethiopia Reconsidered. *Africa: Journal of the International African Institute*, Vol. 69, pp. 485–509.

Pankhurst, A. (2003). Introduction: Dimensions and Conceptions of Marginalisation. In: Freeman D. and Pankhurst A. (Eds.), *Peripheral People: The Excluded Minorities of Ethiopia*. Lawrenceville, NJ: The Red Sea Press, Chapter 1, pp. 1–26.

Paynter, R. (1985). Surplus Flow between Frontiers and Homelands. In: Green, S. and Perfman, S.M. (Eds.), *The Archeology of Frontiers and Boundaries*. Orlando: Academic Press, pp. 163–211.

Portes, A. (1998). Social Capital: Its Origins and Applications in Modern Sociology. *Annual Review of Sociology*, Vol. 24, pp. 1–24.

Portes, A. (2003). Latin American Class Structures: Their Composition and Change During the Neoliberal Era. *Latin American Research Reviews*, Vol. 38, No. 1, pp. 41–82.

Putnam, R. (1995). Bowling Alone: America's Declining Social Capital. *Journal of Democracy*, Vol. 6. No. 1, pp. 65–78.

Putnam, R. (2000). *Bowling Alone: The Collapse and Revival of American Community*. New York: Simon and Schuster.

Putnam, R. (2001). Social Capital, Measurement and Consequences. In: Helliwell, J.F. (Ed.), *The Contribution of Human and Social Capital to Sustained Economic Growth and Well-Being*, Proceedings of an OECD/HRDC Conference (Quebec, March 2000), Ottawa. Ontario, Canada: Human Resources Development Canada, pp. 117–35.

Ruyle, E. (1973). Slavery, Surplus, and Stratification on the North-West Coast: The Ethnoenergetics of an Incipient Stratification System. *Current Anthropology*, Vol. 14, No. 5, pp. 603–31.

Sassen, S. (1991). *The Global City: New York, London, Tokyo*. Princeton, NJ: Princeton University Press.

Sassen, S. (1996a). *Losing Control: Sovereignty in an Age of Globalization*. New York: Columbia University Press.

Sassen, S. (1996b). Whose City Is It? Globalization and the Formation of New Claims. *Public Culture*, Vol. 2, pp. 205–24.

Scott, J.C. (1972). Patron-Client Politics and Political Changes in Southeast Asia. *American Political Science Review*, Vol. 66, pp. 91–113.

Scott, J.C. (1976). *The Moral Economy of the Peasant: Rebellion and Subsistence in South-East Asia*. New Haven, CT: Yale University Press.

Scott, J.C. (1985). *Weapons of the Weak: Everyday Forms of Resistance*. New Haven, CT: Yale University Press.

Scott, J.C. (1990). *Domination and the Arts of Resistance: Hidden Transcripts*. New Haven, CT: Yale University Press.

Scott, J.C. (2009). *The Art of Not Being Governed*. New Haven, CT: Yale University Press.

Sen, N. and Islam, N. (2000). *A Short Study on the Informal Solid Waste Management and the Socio-economic Conditions of the Recycling Unit Workers*. Misereor International.

Shore, C. and Nugent, L. (Eds.) (2002). *Elite Cultures: Anthropological Perspectives*. London and New York: Routledge.

Siisiäinen, M. (2000). *Two Concepts of Social Capital: Bourdieu vs. Putnam*. Paper presented at ISTR Fourth International Conference 'The Third Sector: For What and for Whom?,' Trinity College, Dublin, Ireland. Mimeo.

Straube, H. (1963). *Völker Süd-Aethiopiens 3*. Stuttgart: West-kuschitische Völker.

Todd, D. (1978). The Origins of Outcasts in Ethiopia: Reflections on an Evolutionary Theory. *Abbay*, Vol. 9, pp. 145–58.

Wacquant, L. (2000). The New 'Peculiar Institution': On the Prison as Surrogate Ghetto. *Theatrical Criminology*, Vol. 4, No. 3, pp. 377–89.

Wacquant, L. (2001a). Deadly Symbiosis: When Ghetto and Prison Meet and Mesh. *Punishment and Society*, Vol. 3, pp. 95–134.

Wacquant, L. (2001b). The Penalization of Poverty and the Rise of Neo-Liberalism. *European Journal on Criminology Policy and Research*, Vol. 9, pp. 401–12.

Wacquant, L. (2006 [2009]). Social Insecurity and the Punitive Upsurge. In: Wacquant, L. [Trans. Wacquant, L.], *Punishing the Poor: The Neoliberal Government of Social Insecurity*. Durham NC: Duke University Press, Chapter 1, pp. 1–40.

Wacquant, L. (2007a). Territorial Stigmatisation in the Age of Advanced Marginality. *Thesis Eleven*, Vol. 91, No. 1, pp. 66–77.

Wacquant, L. (2007b). The Place of the Prison in the New Government of Poverty. In: Frampton, M.L., López, I.H. and Simon, J. (Eds.), *After the War on Crime*, New York: New York University Press, pp. 23–36.

Wacquant, L. (2008). The Militarization of Urban Marginalization: Lessons from the Brazilian Metropolis. *International Political Sociology*, Vol. 2, pp. 56–74.

Wacquant, L. (2010a). Urban Desolation and Symbolic Denigration in the Hyperghetto. *Social Psychology Quarterly*, Vol. 73, No. 3, pp. 215–19.

Wacquant, L. (2010b). Crafting the Neoliberal State: Workfare, Prisonfare, and Social Insecurity. *Sociological Forum*, Vol. 25, No. 2, pp. 197–220.

Wacquant, L. (2012). Three Steps to a Historical Anthropology of Actually Existing Neoliberalism. *Social Anthropology*, Vol. 20, No. 1, pp. 66–79.

Index

For Product Safety Concerns and Information please contact our EU representative GPSR@taylorandfrancis.com
Taylor & Francis Verlag GmbH, Kaufingerstraße 24, 80331 München, Germany

www.ingramcontent.com/pod-product-compliance
Ingram Content Group UK Ltd.
Pitfield, Milton Keynes, MK11 3LW, UK
UKHW011020180926
475701UK00004B/844

* 9 7 8 0 3 6 7 5 8 9 7 3 8 *